PUBLIC POLICYMAKING
IN THE AMERICAN STATES

PUBLIC POLICYMAKING IN THE AMERICAN STATES

Jack M. Treadway

PRAEGER SPECIAL STUDIES • PRAEGER SCIENTIFIC

New York • Philadelphia • Eastbourne, UK
Toronto • Hong Kong • Tokyo • Sydney

Library of Congress Cataloging in Publication Data

Treadway, Jack M.
  Public policymaking in the American states.

  Includes bibliographical references and index.
  1. State governments.   2. Policy sciences.
I. Title.   II. Title: Public policy making in the
American states.
JK2431.T74   1985   353.9   85-6498
ISBN 0-03-003783-2 (alk. paper)

Published and Distributed by the
Praeger Publishers Division
(ISBN Prefix 0-275)
of Greenwood Press, Inc.,
Westport, Connecticut

Published in 1985 by Praeger Publishers
CBS Educational and Professional Publishing, a Division of CBS Inc.
521 Fifth Avenue, New York, NY 10175 USA

56789 052 987654321

Printed in the United States of America on acid-free paper

INTERNATIONAL OFFICES

Orders from outside the United States should be sent to the appropriate address listed below. Orders from areas not
listed below should be placed through CBS International Publishing, 383 Madison Ave., New York, NY 10175 USA

Australia, New Zealand
Holt Saunders, Pty. Ltd., 9 Waltham St., Artarmon, N.S.W. 2064, Sydney, Australia

Canada
Holt, Rinehart & Winston of Canada, 55 Horner Ave., Toronto, Ontario, Canada M8Z 4X6

Europe, the Middle East, & Africa
Holt Saunders, Ltd., 1 St. Anne's Road, Eastbourne, East Sussex, England BN21 3UN

Japan
Holt Saunders, Ltd., Ichibancho Central Building, 22-1 Ichibancho, 3rd Floor, Chiyodaku, Tokyo, Japan

Hong Kong, Southeast Asia
Holt Saunders Asia, Ltd., 10 Fl, Intercontinental Plaza, 94 Granville Road, Tsim Sha Tsui East, Kowloon,
Hong Kong

**Manuscript submissions should be sent to the Editorial Director, Praeger Publishers, 521 Fifth Avenue,
New York, NY 10175 USA**

To my parents,
who made everything possible

PREFACE

The motivations for this book were twofold. First, for the past two decades, the comparative analysis of state policymaking has been one of the most active areas of political science research. The time appeared propitious for an attempt at an extensive synthesis of the growing body of empirical studies. Second, I deal with state policy-making in my Public Policy Analysis course. My undergraduate and graduate students have been forced to rely on journal articles during this segment of the course. I felt that a book in this area would be a boon to me and other professors who teach about state policymaking. Whether this book provides either an adequate synthesis or a useful teaching tool is for others to decide.

As is always the case with any major undertaking, a debt of gratitude is owed to others for their assistance. The Research Committee at Kutztown University provided funds to offset the costs associated with writing this book. Carol Dignazio typed the entire manuscript with great speed and accuracy, always meeting deadlines. She also caught many of my mistakes. Truly, this book could not have been produced as quickly or as well without her outstanding efforts. A Kutztown University undergraduate student, Robbin Wingfield, produced the graphics.

The people at Praeger have impressed me with their helpfulness and competence. In particular, I have worked for several months with Tina Nimmons. Tina has been a pleasant voice on the phone as well as the source of much assistance. Stephanie Grant has supervised the production of the finished manuscript in a most efficient manner.

At this point, tradition dictates that the author assign credit for all that is good about his book to others, such as those mentioned above, while accepting responsibility for all that is bad; this I do. However, such an arrangement strikes me as most unfortunate; the reverse would be much more convenient.

Finally, I want to thank my family. As always, my parents encouraged and supported me. My mother thought the book was terrific before I even wrote a single word. In my immediate family, my wife Bonnie was always there; my children, Rachel, Justin, and Tara, provided love while not really understanding what Daddy was up to.

J. M. T.

ACKNOWLEDGMENTS

Table 1.1. Thomas R. Dye, *Politics in States and Policy*, 4th Ed., ©1981, p. 46. Reprinted by permission of Prentice-Hall, Inc., Englewood Cliffs, N.J.

Table 1.2. Kenneth N. Vines, "The Federal Setting of State Politics," in Herbert Jacob and Kenneth N. Vines, ed., *Politics in the American States: A Comparative Analysis*, 3rd ed. Copyright ©1976 by Little, Brown and Company (Inc.). Reprinted by permission.

Table 1.3. Herbert Jacob, "Public Policy in the American States," in Herbert Jacob and Kenneth N. Vines, ed., *Politics in the American States: A Comparative Analysis*, 3rd ed. Copyright ©1976 by Little, Brown and Company (Inc.). Reprinted by permission.

Table 2.1, 5.1, 5.2, and Figures 1.1, 1.3. "Inter-party Competition, Economic Variables, and Welfare Policies in the American States," in *Journal of Politics*. Reprinted by permission of Richard E. Dawson, James A. Robinson, and the Southern Political Science Association.

Tables 2.2, 2.5, 2.8, 5.3 and Figure 1.2. Thomas R. Dye, *Politics, Economics, and the Public: Policy Outcomes in the American States*. Reprinted with permission of Rand McNally and Company, ©1966.

Table 2.3. Austin Ranney, "Parties in State Politics," in Herbert Jacob and Kenneth N. Vines, ed., *Politics in the American States: A Comparative Analysis*, 2nd ed., Copyright ©1971 by Little, Brown and Company (Inc.). Reprinted by permission.

Tables 3.2, 5.10. Thomas R. Dye, *Understanding Public Policy*, 4th Ed., ©1981, p. 361. Reprinted by permission of Prentice-Hall, Inc., Englewood Cliffs, N.J.

Tables 4.1, 4.3, and Figure 4.2. Wayne L. Francis, *Legislative Issues in the Fifty States: A Comparative Analysis*. Reprinted with permission of Rand McNally and Company, ©1967.

Table 4.5, 4.6, 4.7, 5.4. Ira Sharkansky, *Spending in the American States*. Reprinted with permission of Rand McNally and Company, ©1968.

Table 4.4. Wayne L. Francis, "A Profile of Legislator Perceptions of Interest Group Behavior Relating to Legislative Issues in the States." Reprinted by permission of the University of Utah, Copyright Holder.

Figure 4.1. Richard E. Dawson, "Social Development, Party Competition, and Policy," in *The American Party Systems: Stages of Political Development*, ed. William Nisbet Chambers and Walter Dean Burnham. Copyright ©1967 by Oxford University Press, Inc. Reprinted by permission.

CONTENTS

1

THE ANALYSIS OF PUBLIC POLICY

Every citizen is affected by the policy decisions of state governments. Collectively, the American state governments make many more policy decisions than the national government. The states are especially active in such areas as education, welfare, highways, and health care and hospitals. In fiscal 1982, 25 percent of all state governments' direct general expenditures went for education, 24 percent for welfare, 12 percent for highways, and 11 percent for health care and hospitals. These policy areas touch the lives of most citizens. Thus, the quality of education received by a state's young people, the benefits offered to its most unfortunate citizens, the quality of the state's transportation system, and the health care available to a state's citizens depend in large part on the decisions of the state's policymakers.

To be sure, the funds expended by the states in these crucial areas are not always derived from their own revenue sources. Considerable sums of money are provided by the national government, largely through grants-in-aid. In fiscal 1982, federal aid to state governments amounted to $66 billion. This figure represented 20 percent of all state revenues. Typically, grant money is accompanied by federal guidelines circumscribing how the money can be spent. Nonetheless, even if state governments do not always have complete discretion and are not always spending their own money, state policy decisions and expenditures are of extreme importance.

Table 1.1 provides a breakdown of expenditures by level of government during the present century. What is most dramatic is the

TABLE 1.1. A Comparison of the Expenditures of Federal, State, and Local Governments over Seven Decades

	Percentages of Total General Expenditures of Governments in the U.S.[a]		
	Federal[b]	State[c]	Local[c]
1902	35	6	59
1927	31	13	56
1936	50	14	36
1944	91	3	7
1950	64	12	24
1960	62	13	25
1970	64	13	23
1975	61	18	21
1980 est.	58	19	23

[a]Figures may not total correctly because of rounding.
[b]Figures include Social Security and trust fund expenditures.
[c]State payments to local governments are shown as local government expenditures; federal grants-in-aid are shown as federal expenditures.
Source: Thomas R. Dye, *Politics in States and Communities*, 4th ed. (Englewood Cliffs, N.J.: Prentice-Hall, 1981), p. 46.

precipitous decline in the local governmental share of the expenditures. The national government's share has increased by almost two-thirds while the states' share has more than tripled. The national government has replaced the local governments as the biggest spender, while the states are now spending a share almost equal to that of the local governments.

A similar trend emerges if only domestic expenditures are examined (see Table 1.2). Once again, the most dramatic decrease is in the local governments' share, while the national and state shares have increased substantially. The state and local changes have dropped off since the late 1970s due to a combination of a decline in federal aid and the reluctance of financially strapped states and municipalities to increase taxes. Still, the states continue to play a large role in domestic spending, especially in comparison to earlier in this century.

Because of the large sums of intergovernmental aid in the American political system, it is difficult to talk about any policy areas as being the sole domain of any one level of government. Morton Grodzins contends that historically this has always been the case.[1]

He contends that our federal system resembles a marble cake: national, state, and local functions are so intermixed that it is impossible to separate them. All three levels of government share responsibility for the implementation of policies. In most cases, it is more accurate to speak of levels of government having greater or lesser responsibility in a certain policy area than it is to speak of that policy area being the exclusive jurisdiction of a particular level of government.

Nonetheless, expenditures in policy areas do vary considerably by level of government. For example, the national government spends 100 percent of the money in such areas as national defense, space research, and the postal service. National expenditures also amount to 67 percent of the funds spent for housing and urban renewal and 85 percent of the money spent in the area of natural

TABLE 1.2. Percentage Shares of Direct Domestic Public Expenditures by Level of Government

	Spending Level			
	National	State	Local	Total
1902	17	10	73	100
1913	18	11	71	100
1922	18	15	67	100
1938	36	19	45	100
1948	23	26	51	100
1965	33	24	43	100
1972	32	25	43	100
1976	45	22	33	100
1980	48	21	31	100

Source: Kenneth N. Vines, "The Federal Setting of State Politics," in *Politics in the American States: A Comparative Analysis*, 3rd ed., ed. Herbert Jacob and Kenneth N. Vines (Boston: Little, Brown, 1975), p. 17. Compiled from Frederick C. Mosher and Orville F. Poland, *The Costs of American Government: Facts, Trends, Myths* (New York: Dodd, Mead, 1965); *Historical Statistics of the United States* (Washington, D.C.: U.S. Government Printing Office, 1960); *Statistical Abstract of the United States* (Washington, D.C.: U.S. Government Printing Office, 1974), Sec. 15. The 1976 and 1980 data were compiled by the author from data in Advisory Commission on Intergovernmental Relations, *Significant Features of Fiscal Federalism, 1981–82 Edition*, Table 2 (Washington, D.C.: U.S. Government Printing Office, 1983).

resources. On the other hand, state and local governments account for 85 percent of the expenditures for education, 77 percent of the expenditures for highways, and 69 percent of the expenditures for health and hospitals.[2]

Herbert Jacob suggests that the relationship among the various levels of government in the different policy areas can be depicted by categorizing policy outputs according to which level of government predominates and also examining the changing role of the states over the last two decades in each area (see Table 1.3). The state role is increasing in the policy areas of education, law enforcement, water pollution, and air pollution. State activity is declining in the policy areas of mental health, welfare, and transportation. In a majority of the areas, the state role is remaining constant. Jacob points out that there are no policy areas dominated by local governments where the state role is declining.

Many important services that citizens receive are provided by state governments. Policy decisions made at the state level affect the quantity and quality of those services. Most laws that restrict citizen activity are state laws. State officials also issue rules and regulations

TABLE 1.3. Policy Outputs by Level of Government and Recent Changes in the Role of the States

	Output Activity		
	Mostly state	Mostly local	Mostly national
Increasing state activity	Higher education	Primary and secondary education Law enforcement Water pollution	Air pollution
Stable state activity	Public utility regulation Regulation of professions Corrections	Land use control Fire protection Solid waste disposal	Defense Foreign affairs Economic management Housing
Declining state activity	Mental health		Welfare Transportation

Source: Herbert Jacob, "Public Policy in the American States," in *Politics in the American States: A Comparative Analysis*, 3rd ed., ed. Herbert Jacob and Kenneth N. Vines (Boston: Little, Brown, 1976), p. 270.

in such areas as licensing, environmental protection, and utility operations. State courts hear more cases and render more judgments than do federal courts.

State policy decisions also profoundly affect the operation of local governments. State decisions can determine the form of local government as well as the functions performed by, or denied to, local governments, the tax sources available to local governments, and much more. Most intergovernmental aid received by local governments comes from the states. State aid is now the largest source of local revenue. In fiscal 1982, direct state aid totaled $97 billion, or almost 36 percent of state general expenditures. This represents more money than the states received in aid from the national government. State financial aid to local governments includes both money derived from state revenue sources and money passed through to local governments from the national government.

Given the significance of state policy decisions, it is crucial to understand as well as possible how the policymaking process operates at the state level. The type and quality of policies vary among the states. Why do not all states adopt similar policies? How much variation in policy among the states actually exists? What environmental and political system factors account for this variation? Are environmental or political system factors more crucial in explaining policy outputs? Such questions have captured the attention of political scientists during the past two decades. Much empirical data relating to these and similar questions have been collected and analyzed. The purpose of this book is to synthesize that data. I hope that integrating the numerous separate studies of state policymaking will help the student of state government to better understand how state policy is made. The focus will be on empirical studies. The goal is a better understanding of how policy is made, not how it should be made or what policies should be adopted.

The examination of the empirical data will begin in Chapter Two. The remainder of this chapter will be concerned with explaining the key concepts and methodologies employed in the examination of state policymaking. Basically, the state policy research has been comparative, employing some variation of systems theory. After defining the key concepts, I will explain why the comparative approach is useful. Next, systems theory will be explained and the basic systems models employed in comparative state research will be presented. Finally, the weaknesses of these systems models will be discussed.

CONCEPTS ASSOCIATED WITH THE STUDY
OF STATE POLICYMAKING

Public Policy

Public policies are policies made by government officials. Many definitions of public policy have been put forth. Public policy has been defined variously as "the relationship of a government unit to its environment,"[3] "the important things that government makes,"[4] "a 'standing decision' characterized by behavioral consistency and repetitiveness on the part of both those who make it and those who abide by it,"[5] and "whatever governments choose to do or not to do."[6] These and other definitions of public policy share some common characteristics. They suggest that certain values are being stressed. There is also the notion that policymakers consciously have undertaken their actions, that some planning is involved. Moreover, it is implied that policy involves patterned activity; in other words, a policy involves more than a single decision. Another important idea is that policy is being made even when government chooses to do nothing. A decision not to act on a problem is a policy decision, sometimes with consequences more significant than those associated with a decision to act.

A definition is often most useful when it is brief. Therefore, the following definition of public policy will be used in this book: public policy is a series of related governmental decisions to act, or not to act, in a given area of responsibility. This definition assumes that a single decision seldom constitutes a policy. A policy includes specific laws, rules, or regulations as well as subsequent decisions to implement and enforce those laws, rules, or regulations. The policymakers can be both elected and appointed officials. An example of a public policy would be actions by a state's governmental officials increasing the monthly payment to recipients of general assistance.

Policy Outputs

Policy outputs represent the level at which a state is supporting a given policy. Outputs are usually expressed in monetary terms; for example, expenditures per capita. In the example above, the output would be the average monthly payment to general assistance recipients. As will be discussed in more detail later, defining outputs in terms of expenditures poses some problems. Such a definition tells one nothing about who benefits from the policy or if the policy is successful. The amount of money spent on a service also may have no relationship with the quality of that service.

Policy Outcomes

Policy outcomes are the results, intended or unintended, of a given policy. The results of policy decisions are not always those intended by the policymakers. Those who frame public policies are not able to foresee all of the possible consequences of their actions. Let us assume that the policymakers in our example intended to improve the lot of those on welfare. The increased monthly payments might have the effect of enabling recipients to procure more food and better shelter for their families. On the other hand, the increased payments might make welfare more attractive to citizens capable of working. They might decide that the monthly welfare stripend is more attractive than working and cease trying to find jobs. In this case, the policy would have the unintended result of increasing the welfare rolls and costing the state significantly more money. One cannot assume that policies will produce the intended results.

Environment

This concept refers to the soicoeconomic characteristics of the American states. Frequently included are measures of education, income, urbanization, and industrialization. Many policy analysts are of the opinion that such characteristics are prime determinants of the variation in state policy outputs. Additional terms used to convey this concept include ecological variables or socioeconomic variables.

Political System

This concept is employed to refer to an abstraction of the states' political systems. Measures frequently employed to indicate this concept include party competition, voter turnout, and apportionment. Many political scientists contend that political system characteristics are important molders of state policies. Terms used interchangeably with this concept include political variables, system variables, and structural and process variables.

THE COMPARATIVE ANALYSIS OF STATE POLICYMAKING

The comparative approach to the study of political systems dates back to the time of Artistotle.[7] More recently, political scientists in the area of comparative government have compared specific institutions or whole political systems from a cross-national perspective. However, when applied to nations, the comparative approach suffers from a number of limitations. National political systems operate in different historical, cultural, and socioeconomic environments. In addition, institutional arrangements vary. What appear to be identical institutions are often significantly different in practice. For example, in one nation the prime minister might be the chief executive, analogous to our president, while in another nation the prime minister might be a secondary official, possessing less power than the president or premier. In addition to such problems, data collection is often difficult.

The comparative approach has more utility when applied to the American states. The states have many common characteristics. These common characteristics enable the researcher to hold constant many of the variables that pose methodological problems for scholars doing cross-national comparative analysis. Let us examine some of the characteristics held in common by the states.

The American states have a common national history and political culture. Residents of the various states speak the same language. Of greater significance, the states have common institutional arrangements. In each of the states there is an elected governor, an elected legislature, and a court system. Thus, when we compare the office of governor we know we are examining the chief executive of each of the states. With the exception of Louisiana, the states can trace their legal systems back to the Anglo-Saxon common law tradition inherited from England. Because of its French heritage, Louisiana's legal system goes back to the Napoleonic Code.

Each state is characterized by a two-party system: Democrats and Republicans. While the Democratic and Republican parties do not compete on even terms in every state, no state is characterized as having a one-party system. Even in several of the southern states, where the Republicans have been a hopeless minority party for decades, there still exists a Republican party functioning in at least a limited role. Likewise, no state can be characterized as having a multiparty system. Third parties function in many states but traditionally have not been competitive or of long duration.

Each state has a written constitution containing a bill of rights. These constitutions do vary in length and scope of content. The Alabama constitution contains 172,000 words, while the constitutions of Connecticut and Vermont run 8,575 and 6,600 words, respectively. To further portray the constitutional variations, the Georgia constitution presently contains no amendments while the South Carolina constitution has been amended 444 times. Thus, some state constitutions are similar to the United States constitution in that they are very general documents while others go into much detail.

Finally, every state is affected by national events. National economic trends, for example, typically spare no state. Some states may be affected more severely, but inflation or recession touches the citizens of every state.

This detailing of common characteristics is not meant to suggest that the states are identical. The fifty states vary considerably on such measures as industrialization, urbanization, income, and education.[8] Considerable variations also exist in the institutions of government. Nebraska, for example, is the only state with a unicameral legislature and nonpartisan legislative elections. Governors have varying degrees of formal power and state legislative bodies vary in size, power, and method of election. State courts vary in number, name, organization, and powers. Political cultures vary as well among and within the states.[9] The crucial point, however, is that the states share enough in common to facilitate a comparative analysis of policymaking. A researcher can employ measures of social, economic, and political differences to try to account for the different policies produced by basically similar political systems.

Empirical Studies

The literature dealing with the comparative analysis of state policymaking has its origin in both political science and economics.[10]

Important early works on state politics were written by V. O. Key,[11] Duane Lockard,[12] and John Fenton.[13] These political scientists stressed the importance of political system attributes in the determination of policy. In particular, they emphasized the role of two-party competition, voter participation, and apportionment. Naturally enough, these political scientists put forth the notion that variations in political characteristics were crucial in accounting for policy variations.

The economists, on the other hand, stressed the importance of social and economic variables. Some of the more important economists were Solomon Fabricant,[14] Glenn Fisher,[15] and Seymour Sacks and Robert Harris.[16] The variables found to be most important by the economists were per capita income, population density, urbanization, and federal aid.

The political scientists and economists also adopted different methodologies. The political scientists produced regional case studies.[17] The economists employed a comparative approach using multivariate statistical techniques. Thus, the studies produced by the economists had more general applicability.

These two methodologies were joined by Dawson and Robinson in their landmark 1963 article.[18] They employed both socioeconomic and political variables in an attempt to determine the relative ability of the two categories of variables to account for interstate variation in welfare expenditures. The political scientists had stressed the importance of political variables and the economists the importance of socioeconomic variables. Before Dawson and Robinson, however, the two categories of variables had not been employed jointly. The authors' conclusion was that socioeconomic variables were more important.

Probably no piece of research in this area has had as much impact as Thomas Dye's book *Politics, Economics, and the Public.*[19] Dye built on and expanded the work of Dawson and Robinson. Again employing both socioeconomic and political variables in a comparative examination of state policymaking, Dye also concluded that socioeconomic variables were more important than political variables. In the years following these two early works, innumerable studies have been produced. The methodologies have become more sophisticated but the basic question has remained the same: do socioeconomic or political variables account for more of the variation in state policies? The answer most frequently has been that socioeconomic variables are paramount.

Two decades after Dawson and Robinson's work the burden of proof still rests with those trying to make a case for political variables. The preponderance of empirical evidence favors socioeconomic variables over political variables. Of course, this does not mean that politics is insignificant, simply that when socioeconomic and political variables are employed jointly, socioeconomic variables frequently have proved to be more significant. As much as this disturbs some political scientists, it is a fact. However, recent research has significantly enhanced the status of political variables.

MODELS FOR THE ANALYSIS OF POLICYMAKING

Model Building

According to Alan C. Isaak, "theories are used primarily to explain political facts, models to discover them."[20] A model is an abstracted version of reality; for policy analysts, a simplified representation of the policymaking process. For William Riker, the essence of model building "is the creation of a theoretical construct that is a somewhat simplified version of what the real world to be described is believed to be like."[21] Models may be implicit or explicit, written, diagrammatical, or mathematical in form. In addition to providing a simplified version of the political system, models "should order and simplify our thinking about political life. . . ."[22]

As a model is developed, relationships are suggested between the elements in the model. An important function of a model, then, is its ability to suggest hypotheses. The hypothesized relationships posited in the model can be tested with real-world data; to be truly valuable, a model must be testable. If the data confirm the hypotheses, the model does not have to be altered; if the data do not confirm the hypotheses, the model must be altered.[23] In this way, a model aids in the discovery of political relationships.

Dye contends that the basic problem in model building is how much to simplify reality.[24] The utility of a model is its ability to simplify, but a danger is that a vital component of a model will be omitted. At the other extreme, the danger is that the model builder will include superfluous components in the model. The real skill in model building is to know just how much to abstract reality. A decision must be made to include certain variables in the model and to exclude others. Anthony Downs writes of his own model that "it treats a few variables as crucial and ignores others which actually have some influence."[25] Abraham Kaplan expands on this problem:

> Models in behavioral science cannot be expected to fit the data exactly, and for two reasons. . . . First, some of the relevant variables are likely to have been omitted, as well as a great number of factors, which may be individually insignificant but quite important in the aggregate. And second—what is especially true in behavioral science—the variables which are brought into the analysis are not likely to be measured with great exactness. Probabilistic considerations thus assume considerable importance; statistical formulations may usefully be built into the model rather than reserved for the treatment of the relations between the model and the data.[26]

The Systems Model

Political scientists concerned with the analysis of public policy at the state level have developed models with the above characteristics. The models present an abstracted notion of the policymaking process, employ a limited number of independent variables assumed to be important in the explanation of public policy, and suggest relationships among the elements in the models.

The model used by most analysts of public policy is based on the systems framework developed by David Easton.[27] The systems approach envisions government as a political system composed of "an interrelated set of structures and processes that encounter environmental stimuli and respond with 'outputs' of goods, services, and deprivations."[28] The environmental stimuli consist of inputs called supports and demands. Supports are attitudes or actions that promote the system and contribute to its stability. Demands are requests or exhortations for specific actions to be taken by decisionmakers within the system. The political system receives inputs from the environment and converts these into outputs, or policies. In Easton's words:

> What I am depicting here is, in effect, a vast conversion process. In it the inputs of demands and support are acted upon in such a way that it

is possible for the system to persist and to produce outputs meeting the demands of at least some of the members, and retaining the support of most. The system is a way of translating demands and support for a system into authoritative allocations.[29]

Outputs return to the environment in the form of feedback and influence future supports and demands.

The first explicit use of a formal model to examine public policy was by Dawson and Robinson[30] (see Figure 1.1). In their explanation of welfare expenditures in forty-six states they develop a model based on systems analysis with four components: external conditions, political system, political process, and public policy. External conditions are operationalized by measures for wealth, urbanization, and industrialization; political process is operationalized by measures examining three dimensions of party competition; and public policy is operationalized by ranking the states in terms of revenue and welfare expenditures.

FIGURE 1.1. Dawson and Robinson's Model of the Policy Process

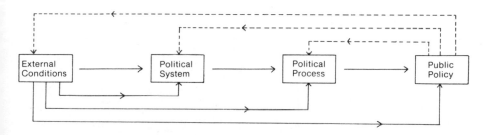

Source: Richard E. Dawson and James A. Robinson, "Inter-party Competition, Economic Variables, and Welfare Policies in the American States," *Journal of Politics* 25 (May 1963): 266.

Several relationships are suggested among the elements in the model. The first assumes that certain external conditions lead to the development of a particular political system, which, in turn, affects the development of the political process, resulting in the development of public policies. The model also assumes that external conditions or political system variables could influence policy without being mediated by the process variables. Finally, external conditions might influence the political process without being mediated by system variables. The model also assumes that policies will feed back and influence the other variables.[31]

One of the most important and influential models has been the one developed by Dye. His model consists of inputs, a political system, and outcomes (outputs according to our terminology). Dye's inputs are variables measuring four dimensions of a state's socioeconomic development: urbanization, industrialization, income, and education. The political system is operationalized by measures for interparty competition, division of two-party control of state government, voting turnout, and state legislative malapportionment. Policy outcomes are fifty-four policy decisions, measured in terms of levels of expenditures by state governments, impacts, and program quality. The model suggests that policy outcomes may be determined by soicoeconomic conditions mediated by political system characteristics, or directly by socioeconomic characteristics of the state. Dye's model assumes that policy outcomes feed back

FIGURE 1.2. A Model for Analyzing Policy Outcomes in American State Politics

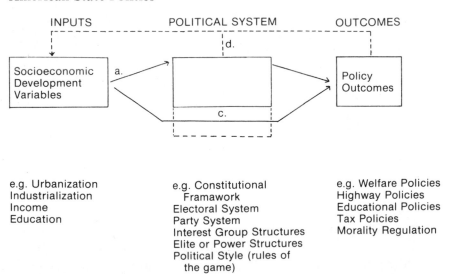

e.g. Urbanization	e.g. Constitutional	e.g. Welfare Policies
Industrialization	Framawork	Highway Policies
Income	Electoral System	Educational Policies
Education	Party System	Tax Policies
	Interest Group Structures	Morality Regulation
	Elite or Power Structures	
	Political Style (rules of	
	the game)	

Source: Thomas R. Dye, *Politics, Economics, and the Public: Policy Outcomes in the American States* (Chicago: Rand McNally, 1966), p. 4.

and influence the political system and the socioeconomic characteristics.[32]

Most work subsequent to Dye's book has employed a model for analysis that is basically a variant of Dye's model. So pervasive is the use of this basic model it has been dubbed "the mainstream model."[33] Most comparative research has been primarily concerned with determining which path in the model is the more important: the path from the environment through the political system to policy outputs or the path directly from the environment to policy outputs. Reduced to its simplest form: is environment or politics more important?

The mainstream model has guided much research and has led to significant increases in our understanding of how policy is made in the states. Nonetheless, the methodological underpinnings of the model have been attacked. We will now consider the criticism directed at the mainstream model.

Criticism of the Mainstream Model

Criticism has been directed at each of the components of the mainstream model.[34] The model has been criticized both for being an inadequate guide for examining policy outputs and for not being faithful to Easton's framework.

The environment, or inputs into the political system, are operationalized in terms of socioeconomic variables. In Easton's model, inputs are supports and demands. Levels of socioeconomic development do not constitute either supports or demands: they are probably factors that influence the level of supports and demands, but they are not such themselves. According to Easton, demands are articulated requests directed to the political system. Exactly how environmental conditions stimulate demands and how those demands subsequently enter the political system are never specified in the model. The perceptions of the citizenry are probably crucial in the transformation of environmental circumstances into demands.[35] The nature of the demands with which policymakers are confronted depends on how individuals and groups view the world around them.

The model implies that similar environmental conditions will produce similar demands. More likely, given the different perceptions of the world that exist, a given environmental situation will produce varying demands. Because of their different backgrounds and biases, different groups of citizens, viewing the same situation, will probably urge government to pursue varying courses of action. Thus, "what enters the political process, the so-called black box, is not a single, unambiguous demand from the environment, but a complex of conflicting demands derived from the differing perceptions that individuals have of the environment."[36] At the other extreme, policymakers in states with different environments could be confronted with similar demands for policy.

The model also fails to account for how demands, once generated, are translated into a form that the political system can understand and act upon. Some type of interest aggregation must take place. Somehow the various conflicting demands must be brokered and presented to the policymakers. The process by which this occurs is never specified.

The mainstream model also assumes that demand is constant across the states. No method is available for distinguishing the level or intensity of demands. It is quite possible that in one state the per pupil expenditure for education is twice what it is in another state because the demand is twice as great. Yet the model does not provide for the possibility of different levels of demand for a given policy. The model also does not recognize that demands can originate within the political system ("withinputs" in Easton's terms) as well as in the environment. All demands do not enter the system from the environment; some are generated within the system.

The mainstream model typically operationalizes the environment with measures of social and economic characteristics. The result is that other crucial factors are often ignored. Munns, for example, cites three additional variables whose inclusion she believes would enhance the ability of the model to help account for political system development and policy outputs: political culture, federal policy, and region.[37] While political culture and region are not precise variables and their merits are subject to debate,[38] their inclusion in the model might prove fruitful.

The mainstream model's abstraction of the political system is generally considered to be deficient on two principal counts. First, the limited number of political variables employed are felt not to portray accurately the political system. Perhaps they are not even the best variables that could be used. The political system variables most commonly employed are measures for party competition, electoral participation, and apportionment. These variables are included largely because previous writers implied that they were important.[39] The attention given to these variables has caused analysts to slight other potentially significant variables. Some of the crucial aspects of the political system receiving scant attention include the governor's relations with his or her party's legislative leaders, the level of legislative party cohesion, the strength of legislative committees, formal sanctions available to the governor, the impact of interest groups on the policymaking process, and the perceptions of the governor, legislators, and bureaucrats. Admittedly, the development of such variables would be exceedingly difficult. But the inclusion of these and similar variables would permit a more realistic conception of the political system.

A second criticism has been that the political system variables employed do not always measure the concepts they are intended to measure. Party competition is a good example. Party competition is usually measured in terms of the two-party share of the vote for governor or the percentage of legislative seats held by each party during a specified time period. Such measures tell one little about the nature of party competition. For example, it is unknown whether the two parties present the electorate with significantly different policy alternatives, whether legislative party competition is close throughout the state or if the relative balance of seats in the legislature simply reflects an equal number of noncompetitive districts controlled by each party, and whether party control of legislative seats translates into partisan votes on policy questions.

Rakoff and Schaefer offer an additional criticism. They correctly point out that every input does not become an output. Some inputs are converted into outputs in the same form in which they entered the political system, some are converted into outputs but in a modified form, and others never become outputs. They take to task the proponents of the mainstream model for not explaining which inputs will fall into each category. Rakoff and Schaefer contend that what needs to be done "is to question clearly what happens to inputs on their way to becoming outputs, why some make it and others do not, and why some are substantially changed while others are simply ratified by the governmental institutions."[40]

The way outputs are conceptualized is also criticized as being inadequate. Most commonly, outputs are defined in terms of per capita expenditures. Such spending data say nothing about why a particular policy was adopted, how the outputs are distributed among the population, the quality of the services delivered, or the impact of the policy. Moreover, some policies are not accurately measured by expenditure data.[41]

Quite often a policy is adopted because more support exists for that policy than for others. Information about how much money is being spent in a given policy area tells one nothing about the relative balance of power among competing groups. Why a given set of interests prevailed is a crucial and interesting political question.

The distribution of a policy is at the heart of the political process. How policy outputs are distributed is also a manifestation of the balance of power within a political system. Simply knowing expenditures per capita gives one little insight into this vital area. For example, let us assume that under an educational policy adopted by a state $300 per pupil will be spent in a fiscal year. That could mean that $300 will be spent on every student in the state or it could mean that some students will have considerably more than that spent on them while others will receive considerably less. Policies with the same levels of expenditures could have decidedly different consequences in practice.

Implicit or explicit in the policy literature is the notion that a higher level of expenditures results in a higher level of service. Such an assumption must be proved. Much impressionistic evidence suggests that might not be the case at all. In fact, there is empirical evidence indicating that gross levels of expenditures do not translate into gross levels of service.[42] Other factors, including the skills and commitment of public servants, are probably of equal importance.

Knowledge about policy impacts cannot be inferred from expenditure data. One must examine how the money is spent and what the results of the expenditures are. The results are often not what was intended.

Furthermore, the expenditure data employed are frequently a combination of state and local spending while the independent variables typically are measures of the state's environment and political system.[43] If local governmental structures or processes, or local environmental conditions, are influential in the determination of spending levels for a specific policy the model will not be able to accurately gauge that influence. The data used to measure the independent and dependent variables are thus not always drawn from the same levels of government.

The use of expenditure data is deficient on two other grounds.[44] First, state policymakers are not free to spend money as they wish. Frequently, more than one half of state revenues are earmarked for a particular agency or program. Most of the remaining revenue is committed to existing programs. Dramatic alterations in a state's budget occur infrequently. Thus, state expenditures do not necessarily reflect the policy priorities of policymakers. Coupled with the evidence that expenditures do not equate with service levels, this forms the nucleus of a good argument against the use of expenditure data. Second, the amount of revenue available and, quite possibly, the level of expenditures depend upon the wealth of the state. While the availability of money does not ordain that policymakers will spend it, it probably is a necessary condition for higher levels of expenditure. Therefore, to use income as an environmental variable and expenditures per capita as a dependent variable is to correlate money with money. If a significant correlation exists, its meaning could be subject to debate.

The strength of the relationships among the independent and dependent variables employed in the model is measured by correlation coefficients. It must be borne in mind that correlation coefficients demonstrate the strength of relationships, not causation. A high coefficient of correlation means that two variables vary together, not that one necessarily causes the other. Causation is difficult to prove. At a minimum, for one variable to be said to cause another the first variable must be a necessary and sufficient determinant of the second and antecedent in time. Causation cannot be asserted when, as is the case with most of the comparative state literature, the studies are cross-sectional, focusing on one point in time. Also, to prove causation, a change in the antecedent variable must produce a concomitant change in the affected variable.

If environmental variables do indeed cause policy outputs, at least two conditions must exist. The environmental variables must be measures of socioeconomic conditions that antedate the policies, and changes in the environmental variables must be accompanied by changes in policy outputs. An extensive study relating changes in environmental variables with changes in policy outputs over time produced little support for the position that environment determines policy.[45] Dyson and St. Angelo employed all the variables that had been reported in the literature and correlated changes in environmental variables with changes in spending between 1960 and 1967. The relationships proved to be very weak. The only environmental variable consistently correlated with the policy measures was per capita income, and that relationship was unstable. The environment did not account for 10 percent of the variance in spending in any instance. The authors contend that the data do not support an interpretation of a causal relationship.

> The data presented here suggest that there may be no real basis for asserting that taxing and spending policies are a function of a state's socio-economic environment. A change in the environment of less privileged states may not lead to comprehensible changes in relative levels of spending.[46]

Compounding the problems of inference is the fact that the relationships cited to make the case for a particular variable or set of variables are often weak. For example, only 16 of 456 simple correlation coefficients reported by Dye between his four measures of the environment and policy outputs explain at least one half of the variations among the states, and only 19 of 54 coefficients of determination indicate that all four environmental variables together account for one half of the variation in policy outputs.[47]

In addition to the specific shortcomings associated with particular components of the model, more general methodological criticisms have been made. Thomas Anton charges that the use of the systems model creates an image of a political system characterized by determinism, stability, and reaction.[48] In reality, such an image is a false one. Cross-sectional studies do no more than give one a picture of the political system at a point in time. That picture may be the correct one for that time, but is quite possibly a distorted view of the system a decade earlier or a decade later. Moreover, the mainstream model suggests that policymakers are virtual prisoners of the environment. The environment sets clear boundaries within which the policymakers must operate; the policymakers merely react to the environment. Political actors have only a limited ability to mold, or react to the environment.

Robert Savage offers a list of shortcomings associated with the comparative approach:

1. atheoretical "theorizing,"
2. unrewarding interpretation,

3. unsound methodology,
4. vacuous conceptualization,
5. wrongheaded conceptualization,
6. presumptuous conceptualization, and
7. inadequate operationalizing of concepts.[49]

He believes that the atheoretical nature of the literature is especially a problem. As Agger has pointed out, political scientists have assumed that anything expressed in a systems framework has a theoretical foundation.[50] All the systems framework tells us, in Agger's words, is that "things hang together in social life."[51] The systems approach only tells us that things are related to each other, not how they are related. What is lacking is a theory explaining how the various elements in the system are linked together.

The mainstream model is also a faulty conceptualization of the systems model because it generally ignores the concept of feedback. Typically, the mainstream model employed will contain a feedback linkage, but this linkage is not subjected to empirical analysis. Only infrequently is the contribution of feedback to the explanation of interstate policy variation detailed. Presumably, feedback affects both environmental and political system variables, but such relationships are not commonly objects of analysis. This leaves one with the impression that influence runs only in one direction: from the environment to policy outputs. This gives rise to what might be referred to as the conveyor belt theory of policy formulation.[52] It is not realistic to think that influence runs only in one direction.

SUMMARY

During the last twenty years many empirical studies of the state policymaking process have been produced. Written by both economists and political scientists, these works have been comparative in nature. Because the American states have many common characteristics, the comparative approach has much utility.

Much of this research has been guided by a basic systems model similar to the one diagrammed in Figure 1.3. Labeled the mainstream model, this model employs measures of the socioeconomic environment, the political system, and policy outputs. The primary objective of the studies has been to compare the relative merits of socioeco-

FIGURE 1.3. A Systems Model of the Policy Process

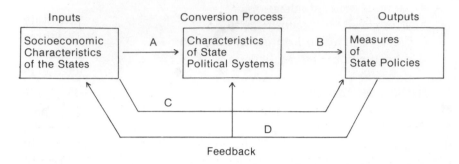

Feedback

nomic and political variables. In terms of linkages in the model, the major emphasis of the research has been directed toward determining whether linkage A–B or linkage C is the more crucial. In other words, are policy outputs better explained by the direct influence of the environment or by the environmental influence mediated by political system characteristics? The bulk of the empirical data have come down on the side of the socioeconomic variables. However, the mainstream model has not been without its critics. I have discussed a number of the shortcomings identified in the model.

Beginning in Chapter Two we will turn our attention to the empirical studies. Chapter Two will focus on the linkage between the socioeconomic characteristics of the states and characteristics of the political system. In Chapter Three our concern will be linkage C–the direct linkage between the environment and policy outputs. Chapter Four will examine the direct influence of the political system on policy outputs, linkage B. Then, in Chapter Five, I will review the studies that have assessed the relative influence of socioeconomic and political variables in accounting for policy outputs. The final chapter will be a discussion of the present state of knowledge of policy-making in the American states.

NOTES

1. Morton Grodzins, *The American System: A New View of Government in the United States* (Chicago: Rand McNally, 1966).

2. Thomas R. Dye, *Politics in States and Communities*, 5th ed. (Englewood Cliffs, N.J.: Prentice-Hall, 1985), p. 64.

3. Robert Eyestone, *The Trends of Public Policy: A Study in Policy Leadership* (Indianapolis: Bobbs-Merrill, 1971), p. 18.

4. Ira Sharkansky, *Public Administration: Agencies, Policies, Politics* (San Francisco: Freeman, 1982), p. 7.

5. Heinz Eulau and Kenneth Prewitt, *Labyrinths of Democracy* (Indianapolis: Bobbs-Merrill, 1973), p. 465.

6. Thomas R. Dye, *Understanding Public Policy*, 4th ed. (Englewood Cliffs, N.J.: Prentice-Hall, 1981), p. 1.

7. This section is influenced by Herbert Jacob and Kenneth N. Vines, "The Study of State Politics," in *Politics in the American States*, 2nd ed., ed. Herbert Jacob and Kenneth N. Vines (Boston: Little, Brown, 1971), pp. 7–10.

8. For an excellent account of the economic and political differences among the states, see Ira Sharkansky, *The United States* (New York: McKay, 1975).

9. See, for example, Daniel J. Elazar, *American Federalism: A View from the States*, 2nd ed. (New York: Crowell, 1972), Chapter 4.

10. Stuart H. Rakoff and Guenther F. Schaefer, "Politics, Policy, and Political Science: Theoretical Alternatives," *Politics and Society* 1 (November 1970): 51–77.

11. V. O. Key, *American State Politics: An Introduction* (New York: Knopf, 1956).

12. Duane Lockard, *New England State Politics* (Princeton, N.J.: Princeton University Press, 1959).

13. John F. Fenton, *People and Parties in Politics* (Glenview, Ill.: Scott, Foresman, 1966).

14. Solomon Fabricant, *Trend of Government Activity in the United States Since 1900* (New York: National Bureau of Economic Research, 1952).

15. Glenn F. Fisher, "Interstate Variation in State and Local Government Expenditures," *National Tax Journal* 17 (March 1964): 57–74.

16. Seymour Sacks and Robert Harris, "The Determinants of State and Local Expenditures and Intergovernmental Flows of Funds," *National Tax Journal* 17 (March 1964): 75–85.

17. V. O. Key, *Southern Politics in State and Nation* (New York: Knopf, 1951); Lockard, *New England State Politics*; and John H. Fenton, *Midwest Politics* (New York: Holt, Rinehart, and Winston, 1966).

18. Richard E. Dawson and James A. Robinson, "Inter-Party Competition, Economic Variables, and Welfare Policies in the American States," *Journal of Politics* 25 (May 1963): 265–89.

19. Thomas R. Dye, *Politics, Economics, and the Public: Policy Outcomes in the American States* (Chicago: Rand McNally, 1966).

20. Alan C. Isaak, *Scope and Methods of Political Science* (Homewood, Ill.: Dorsey Press, 1969), p. 136.

21. William Riker, *The Theory of Political Coalitions* (New Haven: Yale University Press, 1962), p. 7.

22. Dye, *Politics, Economics, and the Public*, p. 2.

23. Ibid.

24. Ibid., pp. 2–3.

25. Anthony Downs, *An Economic Theory of Democracy* (New York: Harper and Row, 1957), p. 3.

26. Abraham Kaplan, *The Conduct of Inquiry* (San Francisco: Chandler, 1964), p. 291.

27. David Easton, *A Framework for Political Analysis* (Englewood Cliffs, N.J.: Prentice-Hall, 1965). For a further discussion by Easton, see *A Systems Analysis of Political Life* (New York: Wiley, 1965), and *The Political System*, 2nd ed. (New York: Knopf, 1971).

28. Brett W. Hawkins, *Politics and Urban Policies* (Indianapolis: Bobbs-Merrill, 1971), p. 11.

29. Easton, *A Framework for Political Analysis*, p. 131.

30. Dawson and Robinson, "Inter-Party Competition."

31. Ibid., p. 266.

32. Dye, *Politics, Economics, and the Public*, pp. 3–5.

33. Joyce Matthews Munns, "The Environment, Politics, and Policy Literature: A Critique and Reformulation," *Western Political Quarterly* 28 (December 1975): 646.

34. This discussion relies heavily on Rakoff and Schaefer; Herbert Jacob and Michael Lipsky, "Outputs, Structure, and Power: An Assessment of Changes in the Study of State and Local Politics," in *Political Science: Advance of the Discipline*, ed. Martin D. Irish (Englewood Cliffs, N.J.: Prentice-Hall, 1968), pp. 220–48; Munns, "The Environment, Politics, and Policy Literature," pp. 646–67; and John H. Fenton and Donald W. Chamberlayne, "The Literature Dealing with the Relationships Between Political Processes, Socioeconomic Conditions and Public Policies in the American States: A Bibliographical Essay," *Polity* 1 (Spring 1969): 388–404.

35. See Rakoff and Schaefer, "Politics, Policy, and Political Science," pp. 61–77.

36. Ibid., p. 66.

37. Munns, "The Environment, Politics, and Policy Literature," pp. 651–53.

38. See, for example, Robert L. Lineberry and Edmund P. Fowler, "Reformism and Public Policy in American Cities," *American Political Science Review* 61 (September 1967): 707; Hawkins, *Politics and Urban Policies*, pp. 40–41; and Hubert M. Blalock, *Causal Inferences in Nonexperimental Research* (Chapel Hill: University of North Carolina Press, 1964), p. 164.

39. Dye, *Politics, Economics, and the Public*, pp. 13–20, 297.

40. Rakoff and Schaefer, "Politics, Policy, and Political Science," p. 57.

41. Richard D. Hofferbert, "State and Community Policy Studies: A Review of Comparative Input-Output Analysis," in *Political Science Annual: An International Review*, ed. James A. Robinson (Indianapolis: Bobbs-Merrill, 1972), p. 37.

42. See Ira Sharkansky, "Government Expenditures and Public Services in the American States," *American Political Science Review* 61 (December 1967): 1066–77.

43. For a discussion of this problem, see Ira Sharkansky, "Economic and Political Correlates of State Government Expenditures: General Tendencies and Deviant Cases," *Midwest Journal of Political Science* 11 (May 1967): 173–92;

and Dennis D. Riley, "Party Competition and State Policy-Making: The Need for a Reexamination," *Western Political Quarterly* 24 (September 1971): 513.

44. See Joel A. Thompson, "Outputs and Outcomes of State Workmen's Compensation Laws," *Journal of Politics* 43 (November 1981): 1130–31.

45. James W. Dyson and Douglas St. Angelo, "A Methodological Problem in the Socio-Economic Interpretation of State Spending," *Policy Studies Journal* (Winter 1973): 131–37.

46. Ibid., p. 135.

47. Ira Sharkansky and Richard I. Hofferbert, "Dimensions of State Policy," in Jacob and Vines, *Politics in the American States*, p. 320.

48. Thomas J. Anton, "The Imagery of Policy Analysis: Stability, Determinism, and Reaction," *Policy Studies Journal* 3 (Spring 1975): 225–33.

49. Robert L. Savage, *The Literature of Systematic Quantitative Comparison in American State Politics: An Assessment* (Philadelphia: Temple University Center for the Study of Federalism, Report No. 11, 1976), p. 10.

50. Ben Agger, "Invisible Politics: Critique of Empirical Urbanism," *Polity* 6 (Summer 1974): 540–51.

51. Ibid., p. 542.

52. Munns, "The Environment, Politics, and Policy Literature," p. 646.

2

THE INFLUENCE
OF THE ENVIRONMENT
ON THE POLITICAL SYSTEM

The mainstream model hypothesizes a direct linkage between the environment and the political system. It suggests that environmental conditions can influence directly the characteristics of a state's political system. Environmental conditions give rise to demands for specific policies. The nature of the demands helps to set the policy agenda acted upon by the state's policymakers The environment also, according to the model, gives shape to the political structures and processes vital to the processing of those demands. A political system is shaped by, and responds to, its environment. The level of party competition, the level of voter turnout, legislative party cohesion, and the formal powers available to the governor, among other political system characteristics, are determined in part by the environment within which the system operates.

In this chapter we will examine the direct linkage between the environment and the political system. Understanding this relationship is crucial if one is later to understand the complex relationships among the environment, political system characteristics, and policy outputs. Income, education, industrialization and urbanization are the variables most frequently employed to operationalize the environment. But other variables have been used in policy studies. I will summarize all of the important relationships that have been discovered.

PARTY COMPETITION

The Democratic and Republican parties do not compete on equal terms in each of the states. Domination to some degree by one of the parties is not uncommon. The parties are really competitive in only about one half of the states. Interparty competition can also vary according to the offices being contested. For example, some states are characterized as being competitive for state offices but noncompetitive for national offices, or vice versa. It is also possible, as witnessed in the southern states, for states to be noncompetitive at both levels but with a different party dominant in state and national elections. Today, the Republican party wins most of the southern electoral votes in presidential elections while the Democrats dominate state elections in the South. Therefore, one must be careful when speaking about party competition. It is crucial to explain what offices are being examined and the time period being studied. Generalizations about interparty competition apply only to the category of elections being examined during a specific time period. The degree of competition for a different set of offices or during the years preceding, or subsequent to, a particular study might be significantly different.

If the object of examination is state policy outputs, the measure of competition should be derived from an examination of state electoral results because state policymakers, not those at the national level, are primarily responsible for the outputs being examined. There have been several attempts to measure the level of state party competition and to relate it to socioeconomic characteristics of the states. All of the studies detailed here have defined party competition in terms of competition for state offices.

One of the first attempts was by Robert Golembiewski.[1] He categorized the states as being one-party states, two-party states, or weak minority-party states. He then examined the relationship between party strength and fifteen "nonpolitical" characteristics. Golembiewski reported statistically significant relationships between party competition and urbanization, population density, population mobility, percentage black, percentage foreign stock, income, education, and industrialization. Specifically, increased competition was associated with greater urbanization, higher population density, greater population mobility, a smaller proportion of blacks, higher income and educational levels, and greater industrialization.[2]

TABLE 2.1. Rank Order Correlations between External Conditions and Interparty Competition

External Conditions	Party Competition Measures		
	Average Percentage of Popular Support for Governor, Senate, and House	Percentage of Times the Predominant Party Has Controlled Units of Government	Percentage of Times Control Has Been Divided between Parties
Per capita income	.71	.65	.73
Urbanization	.58	.54	.56
Industrialization	.59	.48	.57

Source: Richard E. Dawson and James A. Robinson, "Inter-Party Competition, Economic Variables, and Welfare Policies in the American States," Journal of Politics 25 (May 1963): 284.

Dawson and Robinson offer further support for Golembiewski's findings. They report significant relationships among their three measures of party competition and income, urbanization, and industrialization (see Table 2.1). In every case, the relationship between per capita income and the dependent variable is higher than comparable correlations for the other independent variables.[3]

Sharkansky finds that income and urbanization are positively correlated with party competition, with income being the stronger variable.[4] Interestingly, when Sharkansky tests the relationship between region and competition while controlling for income and urbanization, he finds region to be a more significant variable.[5]

Dye finds greater party competition in wealthier states with better-educated populations (see Table 2.2).[6] Conversely, less party competition exists in poorer states with less well-educated citizens. These relationships are strongest in gubernatorial elections. A weaker relationship exists between urbanization and competition in state senate elections. Dye notes that neither party is advantaged by income and educational characteristics. Both one-party Republican and one-party Democratic states contain residents with lower income and educational levels. Higher levels of income and education foster increased competition rather than contributing to the domination of either party.

Similar findings are reported in a study examining the correlation between environmental variables and gubernatorial election results.[7] Income and education are much more strongly related to competition in gubernatorial elections than industrialization and urbanization. However, the strongest correlation is a negative relationship between percentage black and party competition. Percentage black is positively correlated with Democratic party strength. This is a result of large concentrations of blacks in the southern states.

Almost identical findings are reported by Casstevens and Press.[8] Their measures of competition correlated significantly with wealth and education but very weakly and erratically with urbanization and industrialization.

One of the most widely employed measures of party competition is the index developed by Austin Ranney. On the basis of competition for governor and legislative seats, a numerical index score is computed for each state. Depending on the score, the state is placed in one of five categories of party competition: one-party Democratic or Republican, modified one-party Democratic or Republican, or two-party. A profile of the different categories is presented in Table 2.3. The two-party states are more urbanized and have citizens with higher incomes who are more likely to be union members and to be engaged in nonagricultural occupations. Two-party states also have higher proportions of foreign stock and lower proportions of nonwhites.[9]

TABLE 2.2. The Relationship between Economic Development and Party Competition

	Economic Development			
	Urbanization	Industrialization	Income	Education
Party competition				
Lower houses	.26	.00	.52*	.57*
Upper houses	.30*	.03	.51*	.50*
Governorships	.29	.18	.66*	.62*

Note: Figures are simple correlation coefficients for forty-eight states; an asterisk indicates a statistically significant relationship.

Source: Thomas R. Dye, *Politics, Economics, and the Public: Policy Outcomes in the American States* (Chicago: Rand McNally, 1966), p. 58.

TABLE 2.3. Social and Economic Characteristics of States, by Degree of Competitiveness

Characteristics	One-Party Democratic	Modified One-Party Democratic	Two-Party	Modified One-Party Republican
Number of states	7	10	28	5
Percentage of population urban	53	57	68	46.5
Percentage of population living in cities of over 100,000	17	20	22	5
Percentage of blacks in population	29	14.5	4	1
Percentage of foreign stock in population	3	6	23	22
Percentage of Roman Catholics among church members	16	21	44	42
Median income	$3,884	$4,764	$5,999	$4,920
Percentage of labor force in agriculture	11	8	7	17
Percentage of labor force in manufacturing	20	19	22.5	17

Source: Austin Ranney, "Parties in State Politics," in Politics in the American States: A Comparative Analysis, 2nd ed., ed. Herbert Jacob and Kenneth N. Vines (Boston: Little, Brown, 1971), p. 90.

Sarah McCally Morehouse approaches the concept of competition from a different perspective. Employing factor analysis to examine competition for governor, she identifies two important measures: integration and income distribution. Morehouse explains the dimension tapped by the integration factor.

The variables clustered around this concept are characteristics of modern affluent cultures. In contrast to a measure of the degree of industrialization of an economy, this dimension measures a postindustrial type of economic activity. The variables that are highly associated with integration are wealth and degree of professionalism. States that score high on integration have a disproportionate share of professionals such as doctors or public administrators and are disproportionately middle-class; they are marked by high degrees of education, literacy, and media circulation. Finance and insurance as opposed to heavy industry distinguish this type of socioeconomic development. As with industry, the finance and insurance are concentrated in urban areas.[10]

The second variable, called the Gini coefficient, measures how equally income is distributed within a state. The coefficient ranges in value from zero to one. A value of zero indicates perfect equality while a value of one indicates perfect inequality.

In Morehouse's analysis, the fifty states are broken down into five groups according to the level of party competition (see Table 2.4). The first three groups are more competitive than are the last two. The more competitive groups contain states that tend to be wealthier, more professional, and have a more equitable distribution of income.

Within the first three groups of states are all the states with great wealth, middle-class economies and large numbers of minorities such as Massachusetts, New York, California, New Jersey, and Connecticut. High also on this list are Delaware, Illinois, Rhode Island, Washington, Hawaii, Colorado, and Arizona. The second two groupings of states would tend to confirm our notions that states that have a large proportion of minorities, and an urban population, and in which there is great wealth are states that would provide the same bases for two-party competition as those that divide the parties on the national level.[11]

Still, these are simply tendencies, as within each group there is a state or two that does not perfectly fit the pattern. Dye also repeats that competition is greater when income distribution is more equal.[12]

The strongest competition exists within the nine states that constitute the first group. These states are characterized by dissimilar degrees of wealth and population density. However, in seven of the states income is more equally distributed than in the rest of the nation. This leads Morehouse to conclude that "apparently, income distribution is even more predictive of the competitive nature of state politics than the integration factor."[13]

TABLE 2.4. The Fifty States According to Competition,
Integration, and Income Distribution

Name of States	Average Index of Competition 1956–70	Average Index of Integration 1970	Average Index of Income Distribution 1970
Delaware, Illinois, Wisconsin, Idaho, Maine, Minnesota, New Mexico, West Virginia, Montana	5.3 (most)	–0.07	0.350
Indiana, Kentucky, Michigan, Pennsylvania, Rhode Island, Washington, North Dakota, Alaska, South Dakota, Oregon, Hawaii, Kansas, Massachusetts, New York	8.6	0.26	0.353
Iowa, Colorado, Nebraska, Arizona, New Hampshire, Wyoming, California, New Jersey, Connecticut, Vermont	11.5	0.72 (most)	0.345 (most)
Utah, Nevada, North Carolina, Ohio, Missouri, Virginia, Oklahoma, Maryland, Florida	17.5	0.002	0.361
Arkansas, Texas, Tennessee, Mississippi, Georgia, South Carolina, Alabama, Louisiana	52.7 (least)	–1.28 (least)	0.394 (least)
Mean	17.4	0.00	0.359

Source: Sarah McCally Morehouse, State Politics, Parties and Policy (New York: Holt, Rinehart and Winston, 1981), p. 66.

VOTER TURNOUT

The level of electoral participation in the United States is not impressive. Only slightly more than 50 percent of the eligible voters have voted in recent presidential elections. Turnout in off-year congressional elections averages about 40 percent. At the state level, turnout frequently fails to reach even these levels. Between 40 to 45 percent of eligible voters usually participate in elections to choose statewide officials. These aggregate figures mask significant variations among the states, however. Average turnout in presidential elections varies from slightly over 42 percent in South Carolina to slightly under 68 percent in Minnesota. Turnout in gubernatorial elections averages 66 percent among the most competitive states in Morehouse's study but only 29 percent among the least competitive states.[14] What environmental factors account for this variation?

One study of interstate variation in presidential election turnout stresses socioeconomic characteristics.[15] Race, age, income, and education explain approximately 53 percent of the variation in turnout among the states. Turnout is higher in states with older, better-educated citizens with higher incomes, and fewer nonwhites.

This general pattern is reinforced by Dye's research. Income and education are the environmental variables with the strongest association with voter participation (see Table 2.5). Urbanization is weakly correlated with turnout, while the relationship between industrialization and participation is minimal. The levels of income and education of a state's citizens are apparently of greater importance than either urbanization or industrialization in accounting for variations in turnout.

As was the case with competition, income and urbanization are positively correlated with turnout in Sharkansky's study.[16] Once again, however, regionalism turns out to be more influential than either income or urbanization.

In a separate study, Sharkansky reports an association between turnout and a scale based on Elazar's designations of political culture in the states.[17] As hypothesized, turnout is higher and suffrage restrictions are more lenient in states that score high on moralism;

TABLE 2.5. The Relationship between Economic Development
and Voter Participation

Voter Participation	Economic Development			
	Urbanization	Industrialization	Income	Education
Gubernatorial, 1954–1964	.18	.05	.52*	.49*
Congressional, 1958	.21	.08	.61*	.59*
Congressional, 1962	.26	.10	.66*	.63*

Note: Figures are simple correlation coefficients for the fifty states; an asterisk indicates a statistically significant relationship.

Source: Thomas R. Dye, *Politics, Economics, and the Public: Policy Outcomes in the American States* (Chicago: Rand McNally, 1966), p. 62.

the opposite is true of states that score high on traditionalism. These relations hold when controls are imposed for income, urbanization, and region.

Morehouse's measure of income distribution is strongly correlated with the percentage of voters in gubernatorial elections. Turnout is greater when income is more equally distributed.[18] Income and education are found by Hofferbert to be more crucial than urbanization and industrialization. Percentage black is strongly associated with low turnout.[19]

FORMAL POWERS OF THE GOVERNOR

Governors have a number of political resources at their disposal with which to influence the policy process. Some are informal powers, such as their standing within their party, their ability to influence legislators' political careers, and their ability to invoke electoral sanctions against legislators. Such resources vary with the dispositions and political acumen of individual governors. As such, they are difficult to measure and compare. However, governors also have formal powers. Most notable among these are tenure potential, budgetary discretion, appointive power, and veto power. Joseph

Schlesinger has devised an index to measure these powers.[20] Each state's governor is ranked on each of the four formal powers as well as on an overall index incorporating each of the specific powers. Schlesinger finds that greater formal power is available to governors in larger, more urban states. He suggests that as the complexity of a state increases, the governor requires greater powers to deal with problems.[21]

Hofferbert reports modest correlations between Schlesinger's index and a state's level of income and urbanization. A weak relationship exists between the index and industrialization.[22]

Morehouse introduces some additional variables into the examination of formal powers and uncovers some interesting relationships. Contrary to Hofferbert's findings, she reports no relationship at all between industrialization and formal power.[23] Her integration factor is positively related to Schlesinger's index.[24] The Gini index measuring income distribution is negatively associated with formal power. A more equal distribution of income is associated with greater formal power for the governor.[25]

STRENGTH OF INTEREST GROUPS

Interest groups are strong when they are able to influence the determination of policy. In a strong interest group state the dominant group, or groups, is able to tailor policy to its liking. Conversely, in a weak interest group state, interest groups are relatively unsuccessful in determining policy outputs.

The strength of interest groups varies according to the socioeconomic characteristics of the states. Interest groups are characterized as being strong in states that are less urbanized, less industrialized, and poorer. Weak interest group states possess the opposite characteristics.[26] Rural, poorer, less industrialized states tend to have less diversified economies. In such a situation, it is more likely that one or a few economic interests will be able to dominate the policy process. The lack of diversity guarantees less opposition for these groups. When there are more groups competing it is also possible for policymakers to play off one group against another.

In a more extensive examination of the link between environment and interest group strength, Morehouse offers further support for this line of reasoning. Her data show that "in rural, sparsely populated states, a single large company, corporation, or interest group may wield great amounts of power in that state's political system. On the other hand, interest groups appear to have somewhat less impact on public officials in systems containing a diversified economy and large numbers of groups and organizations."[27]

According to Morehouse, weak interest group states are predominately middle class. Educational and literacy levels are higher and income is more equally distributed (see Table 2.6).[28]

TABLE 2.6. Interest Groups' Strength by Economic Background

Economic Strength	State Pressure-Group Strength		
	Weak (10)	Moderate (18)	Strong (22)
Average index of integration	.78 (high)	.20	-.52 (low)
Average Gini index of income distribution	.34 (high)	.35	.37 (low)

Source: Sarah McCally Morehouse, *State Politics, Parties, and Policy* (New York: Holt, Rinehart and Winston, 1981), p. 113.

LEGISLATIVE PROFESSIONALISM

According to John Grumm, a professional legislature is one in which

> members and their committees are well staffed; good informational services are available to them; a variety of services and aids, such as bill drafting and statutory revision, are maintained and well supported; the legislators themselves are well paid, tend to think of their legislative jobs as full time or close to it, and regard their legislative role as a professional one.[29]

Grumm developed a professionalism index based on compensation, length of sessions, expenditures for legislative services and operations, and a legislative services score. A more detailed ranking of the states was produced by the Citizens Conference on State Legislatures.[30] This group's concern was the measurement of legislative capability (professionalism, to use Grumm's term). The state legislatures were ranked according to a number of criteria under five general categories: functional, accountable, informed, independent, representative. The states were rank ordered for each characteristic and an overall rank was assigned on the basis of each state's rank on the separate measures.

More urbanized states with wealthier, better-educated populations score higher on the Citizens Conference overall ranking (see Table 2.7). The states are characterized by a political culture that encourages innovation, participation, and governmental activism. In addition to having more professional legislatures, these states also have governors with stronger formal powers, strong electoral and legislative parties, and strong local governments. Population size, population density, and industrialization are not associated with legislative professionalism. Regionally, legislatures in the north central states score higher while those in the southern states score lower.[31]

Grumm finds that urbanization has the strongest influence on his index, explaining 45 percent of the variation. Economic affluence has no impact at all.[32] Hofferbert measures the association between environment and legislative professionalism using Grumm's index and discovers moderate correlations with income, urbanization, and industrialization.[33] Wealthier, more urbanized, more industrialized states are found to have more professional legislatures. States scoring higher on Grumm's index also have been found by Morehouse to be those with more wealth, higher levels of education, more urban areas, and more citizens in professional occupations.[34] Industrialization is also positively correlated with professionalism, as is a more equal distribution of income.[35]

Using a complex causal model, Asher and Van Meter find urbanization to be related to legislative professionalism.[36] Phillip Roeder modifies the relationship between the environment and professionalism developed by others.[37] His environmental variables are measures of socioeconomic change and inequality. He contends that the environmental variables only indirectly influence professionalism. Socioeconomic change and inequality are mediated by executive reform. Roeder postulates that "through regular contacts the legislature will perceive and respond to the increased professionalism and power of the executive branch by attempting to change its own structures and procedures."[38]

Uslaner and Weber document a negative association between industrialization heterogeneity and professionalism and a positive asso-

TABLE 2.7. Rank Order by State for the FAIIR Criteria

Overall Rank	State	Functional	Accountable	Informed	Independent	Representative
1	Calif.	1	3	2	3	2
2	N.Y.	4	13	1	8	1
3	Ill.	17	4	6	2	13
4	Fla.	5	8	4	1	30
5	Wis.	7	21	3	4	10
6	Iowa	6	6	5	11	25
7	Haw.	2	11	20	7	16
8	Mich.	15	22	9	12	3
9	Nebr.	35	1	16	30	18
10	Minn.	27	7	13	23	12
11	N.M.	3	16	28	39	4
12	Alaska	8	29	12	6	40
13	Nev.	13	10	19	14	32
14	Okla.	9	27	24	22	8
15	Utah	38	5	8	29	24
16	Ohio	18	24	7	40	9
17	S.D.	23	12	16	16	37
18	Ida.	20	9	29	27	21
19	Wash.	12	17	25	19	39
20	Md.	16	31	10	15	45
21	Pa.	37	23	23	5	36
22	N.D.	22	18	17	37	31
23	Kan.	31	15	14	32	34
24	Conn.	39	26	26	25	6
25	W. Va.	10	32	37	24	15
26	Tenn.	30	44	11	9	26
27	Ore.	28	14	35	35	19
28	Colo.	21	25	21	28	27
29	Mass.	32	35	22	21	23
30	Maine	29	34	32	18	22
31	Ky.	49	2	48	44	7
32	N.J.	14	42	18	31	35
33	La.	47	39	33	13	14
34	Va.	25	19	27	26	48
35	Mo.	36	30	40	49	5
36	R.I.	33	46	30	41	11
37	Vt.	19	20	34	42	47
38	Tex.	45	36	43	45	17
39	N.H.	34	33	42	36	43
40	Ind.	44	38	41	43	20
41	Mont.	26	28	31	46	49
42	Miss.	46	43	45	20	28
43	Ariz.	11	47	38	17	50
44	S.C.	50	45	39	10	46
45	Ga.	40	49	36	33	38
46	Ark.	41	40	46	34	33
47	N.C.	24	37	44	47	44
48	Del.	43	48	47	38	29
49	Wyo.	42	41	50	48	42
50	Ala.	48	50	59	50	41

Source: The Citizens Conference on State Legislatures, *State Legislatures: An Evaluation of Their Effectiveness* (New York: Praeger, 1971), p. 40.

ciation between an attentive public (as measured by newspaper readership) and professionalism.[39] Apparently, the effectiveness of the legislative institution is contingent to some extent on the attitudes of the citizenry.

According to Douglas Rose, legislative professionalism is primarily the result of population size and urbanization.[40] Of the two influences, population size is the more important. Larger, more urbanized states have the resources necessary to support a more professional legislature and, perhaps, greater needs that require a more capable legislative body. In addition, Rose opines, "Urbanization promotes role specialization in politics as elsewhere, leading to a full-time specialized law-making body, composed of full-time legislators, full-time staff, etc. The urbanization makes possible the specialization which makes possible professionalism."[41]

LEGISLATIVE APPORTIONMENT

Before the Supreme Court's landmark *Baker v. Carr* decision in 1962, American state legislatures were extremely malapportioned. In forty-seven of the ninety-nine statehouses the largest district was ten times the smallest district. In nine of the houses the ratio was greater than 100 to 1.[42] State legislatures had not been faithful in redistricting every ten years to reflect population movement. The result was that rural areas were overrepresented. As state populations were moving into urban areas, legislative seats were not being reassigned to these areas. This rural advantage in the legislature was blamed for many undesirable pieces of legislation, a number of which had an adverse effect on urban residents. Malapportionment was believed to bias the policymaking process.

The limited evidence available suggests that apportionment is only minimally affected by social and economic conditions. Dye reports that urban, industrial states with higher income levels give better representation to urban areas (see Table 2.8).[43] However, as Dye states,

> there is no relationship between economic development and malapportionment in the technical sense. There are no significant correlations between the index of representativeness or the apportionment score and any of the socioeconomic measures. The legislatures of rural farm

TABLE 2.8. The Relationship between Economic Development and Malapportionment of State Legislatures

	Economic Development			
	Urbanization	Industrialization	Income	Education
Index of representativeness	-.24	-.19	-.21	-.19
Index of underrepresentation	.27	.33*	.36*	-.06
Apportionment score	.01	.14	.14	.13

Note: Figures are simple correlation coefficients for the fifty states; an asterisk indicates a statistically significant relationship.

Source: Thomas R. Dye, *Politics, Economics and the Public: Policy Outcomes in the American States* (Chicago: Rand McNally, 1966), p. 68.

states are just as likely to be unrepresentative in the technical sense as the legislatures of urban industrial states.[44]

Sharkansky found weak and inconsistent associations between legislative apportionment and economic characteristics.[45] When region is employed as a control variable, however, a positive relationship emerges between economic development and apportionment.[46]

SUMMARY

The direct linkage between the environment and the political system was examined in this chapter. Evidence was examined that supports the existence of such a linkage. The structures and processes of state government do indeed differ when environmental configurations differ. One must be cautious in interpreting the data, however. The available empirical data are not consistent. The associations between environmental variables and political system characteristics are not always of identical strength in different studies; indeed, different studies examining the relationship between the same environmental and political system variables occasionally will arrive at very different conclusions. But the disparities are not enough to obviate the existence of an environmental influence on the characteristics of the political system.

TABLE 2.9. Summary of Relationships between Environmental Variables and Political System Characteristics

Environmental Variables	Political System Characteristics				
	Party Competition	Voter Turnout	Formal Powers	Interest-Group Strength	Legislative Professionalism
Urbanization	Positive		Positive	Negative	Positive
Industrialization	Positive			Negative	Positive
Income	Positive	Positive	Positive	Negative	Positive
Education	Positive	Positive			Positive
Percentage black	Negative	Negative			
Population size			Positive	Negative	Positive
Morehouse's integration factor	Positive		Positive	Negative	Positive
Income distribution (equality)	Positive	Positive	Positive	Negative	Positive

Table 2.9 summarizes what is known about the impact of the environment on the political system. The environmental variables listed are some of the more important variables that have been related to political system characteristics. Not every environmental variable that has been linked with a political system characteristic appears. The table indicates whether the relationship is positive or negative—that is, the relationship supported by the bulk of the data. It does not always mean that no contrary evidence exists, merely that the preponderance of the data support such a relationship. Apportionment is not included among the political system characteristics because there is so little support for a relationship between the quality of legislative apportionment and environmental factors.

An understanding of the relationship between the environment and political system characteristics is important. In Chapter Four we will examine the linkage between the political system and policy outputs. There is evidence that political system characteristics do influence policy outputs. But such relationships are complicated by the fact that political system characteristics are influenced by the environment. Is it not possible that environment influences both political system characteristics and policy outputs? That is a question that has frequently been asked by political scientists in recent years, and most often the answer has been affirmative. If one is to be able to deal intelligently with that more complicated issue, a basic understanding of the association between the environment and political system characteristics is essential.

NOTES

1. Robert Golembiewski, "A Taxonomic Approach to State Political Party Strength," *Western Political Quarterly* 11 (September 1958): 494–513.
2. Ibid., p. 511.
3. Richard E. Dawson and James A. Robinson, "Inter-Party Competition, Economic Variables, and Welfare Policies in the American States," *Journal of Politics* 25 (May 1963): 284.
4. Ira Sharkansky, "Economic Development, Regionalism, and State Political Systems," in *State and Urban Politics: Readings in Comparative Public Policy*, ed. Richard I. Hofferbert and Ira Sharkansky (Boston: Little Brown, 1971), pp. 138–40.
5. Ibid., pp. 146–47.
6. Thomas R. Dye, *Politics, Economics, and the Public: Policy Outcomes in the American States* (Chicago: Rand McNally, 1966), pp. 57–58.

7. Richard I. Hofferbert, "State and Community Policy Studies: A Review of Comparative Input-Output Analyses," in *Political Science Annual: An International Review*, ed. James A. Robinson (Indianapolis: Bobbs Merrill, 1972), p. 31.

8. Thomas W. Casstevens and Charles Press, "The Context of Democratic Competition in American State Politics," *American Journal of Sociology* 68 (March 1963): 536–43.

9. Austin Ranney, "Parties in State Politics," in *Politics in the American States: A Comparative Analysis*, 3rd ed., ed. Herbert Jacob and Kenneth N. Vines (Boston: Little, Brown, 1976), pp. 64–65.

10. Sarah McCally Morehouse, *State Politics, Parties and Policy* (New York: Holt, Rinehart and Winston, 1981), pp. 64–65.

11. Ibid., p. 65.

12. Thomas R. Dye, "Income Inequality and American State Politics," *American Political Science Review* 63 (March 1969): 157–62.

13. Morehouse, *State Politics*, p. 67.

14. Ibid., p. 80.

15. Jae-On Kim et al., "Voter Turnout in the American States: Systematic and Individual Component," *American Political Science Review* 69 (March 1975): 107–23.

16. Sharkansky, pp. 138–40.

17. Ira Sharkansky, "The Utility of Elazar's Political Culture," *Polity* (Fall 1969): 66–83.

18. Morehouse, *State Politics*, p. 81; Dye, "Income Inequality," pp. 160–61.

19. Hofferbert, "State and Community Policy Studies," p. 31.

20. Joseph A. Schlesinger, "The Politics of the Executive," in *Politics in the American States*, 2nd ed., ed. Herbert Jacob and Kenneth N. Vines (Boston: Little, Brown, 1971), pp. 210–37.

21. Ibid., pp. 231–33.

22. Hofferbert, "State and Community Policy Studies," pp. 27–28.

23. Morehouse, *State Politics*, pp. 250–51.

24. Ibid., p. 364.

25. Ibid., p. 416; and Dye, "Income Inequality," pp. 160–61.

26. L. Harmon Zeigler and Hendrik van Dalen, "Interest Groups in State Politics," in Jacob and Vines, 3rd ed., pp. 94–95.

27. Morehouse, *State Politics*, pp. 112–13.

28. Ibid.; and Dye, "Income Inequality," pp. 158–59.

29. John G. Grumm, "The Effects of Legislative Structure on Legislative Performance," in Hofferbert and Sharkansky, p. 309.

30. The Citizens Conference on State Legislatures, *State Legislatures: An Evaluation of Their Effectiveness* (New York: Praeger, 1971).

31. Ibid., p. 72.

32. Grumm, "Effects of Legislative Structure," pp. 318–20.

33. Hofferbert, "State and Community Policy Studies," pp. 27–28. He also finds that the factor "industrialization" is positively related to professionalism in *The Study of Public Policy* (Indianapolis: Bobbs-Merrill, 1974), pp. 187–88.

34. Morehouse, pp. 303–4, 364.

35. Ibid., p. 416.

36. Herbert Asher and D. Van Meter, *Determinants of Public Welfare Policies: A Causal Approach* (Beverly Hills: Sage Professional Papers in American Politics, vol. 1, series no. 04–009, 1973). \

37. Phillip W. Roeder, "State Legislative Reform: Determinants and Policy Consequences," *American Politics Quarterly* 7 (January 1979): 51–69.

38. Ibid., p. 57.

39. Eric M. Uslaner and Ronald E. Weber, "The 'Politics' of Redistribution: Toward a Model of the Policy-Making Process in the American States," *American Politics Quarterly* 3 (April 1975): 130–170.

40. Douglas Rose, "Citizen Preference and Public Policy in the American States: A Causal Analysis of Nondemocracy," in *Perspective on Public Policy-Making*, ed. William B. Gwyn and George C. Edwards III (New Orleans: Tulane University, 1975), pp. 53–94.

41. Ibid., p. 64.

42. Dye, *Politics, Economics, and the Public*, pp. 63–64.

43. Ibid., p. 68.

44. Ibid.

45. Sharkansky, "Economic Development," p. 140.

46. Ibid., p. 147.

3

THE INFLUENCE
OF THE ENVIRONMENT
ON POLICY OUTPUTS

A direct linkage between the environment and policy outputs is assumed in the mainstream model. By some process, supports and demands can be translated into outputs without the intervention of the political system. Apparently, if the model correctly abstracts the policymaking process, environmental conditions have a direct impact on policy outputs. This chapter will examine that linkage.

ESTABLISHING THE LINKAGE
BETWEEN ENVIRONMENT AND POLICY

The writings of several economists were instrumental in identifying environmental variab'es as determinants of policy outputs. The initial effort was by Solomon Fabricant.[1] Employing three variables—per capita income, population density, and percentage urban—in a regression equation, he was able to explain 72 percent of the variation in per capita state and local governmental general expenditures for 1942. Employing the same variables, Glenn Fisher was able to explain 53 percent of the variation in 1957 expenditures.[2] Sacks and Harris also were able to account for 53 percent of the variation in 1960 state and local expenditures using Fabricant's variables.[3] Using two of Fabricant's variables plus five others, Fisher accounted for 65 percent of the 1960 variation in governmental expenditures.[4] Dye updated Sacks and Harris's research employing the three variables initially used by Fabricant and found that they accounted for

62 percent of total state and local spending in 1970 and 41 percent in 1980.[5]

The relationship discovered by Fabricant still exists, but the magnitude has been reduced. The decline in the explanatory ability of per capita income, population density, and percentage urban is generally attributed to the increase in federal grants-in-aid. We will examine the influence of federal aid below.

NEEDS VERSUS RESOURCES

The work of the economists, as well as that of Dye, has established a linkage between the environment and policy outputs. What is not clear, however, is exactly how the environment and policy are linked together. Sharkansky identifies two contradictory modes of linkage between the environment and policy.[6] The first he refers to as the resource-policy linkage. This mode assumes that demand for policy is constant. Then, according to Sharkansky, "The resources of rich and poor states either permit or do not permit generous levels of public policy, and explain the service differentials between them."[7] The other linkage is labeled the need–policy linkage. This mode operates "in a contrasting fashion so that policy-makers respond to the needs for service that are associated with low-resource conditions. Public officials in low-income states may tax their citizens with unusual severity to provide a desired level of services."[8] Sharkansky tests the relative merits of the two types of linkage in explaining the distribution of benefits in five welfare programs within thirty-six states.

Sharkansky finds support for both linkages, although the resource linkage is the more prevalent. Interestingly, in seven of the eight examples of need–policy linkage, policymakers appear to be responding to the needs of residents of low-income counties. The highest welfare payments in these states are made in the poorest counties.

Sharkansky's work should caution one against assuming that the linkage between the environment and policy outputs is a simple one. His data substantiate the existence of the resource–policy and need–policy linkages; he also finds evidence of a linkage combining elements of both. Perhaps other linkages exist as well. The linkage between the environment and policy is not consistent among the American states.

PUBLIC OPINION

Democratic theory assigns an important role to public opinion. Elected officials are to carry out the expressed wishes of the citizenry, especially if those wishes are expressed by a majority of the citizens. Majority rule is almost synonymous with democracy. Political decisions are judged as being good or bad depending on how closely they correspond to public opinion. Therefore, an important question is: how closely do public policies correspond with public opinion in the American states?

There is every reason to assume a lack of congruence between policy outputs and public opinion. First, given the lack of political information and interest among the public, there will be many issues for which no public opinion exists. Second, even if opinions exist they must be conveyed to policymakers. Since few citizens regularly contact their elected officials, it is quite possible that opinions will not be transmitted to the policymakers. A frequent complaint of legislators is that they hear little about policy from their constituents. Those who do contact elected officials are usually those who feel most strongly about a particular issue, and thus are unrepresentative of the general public. Third, even if policymakers hear from the public they may choose to ignore what they hear. Finally, because the public is generally uninformed about the policy attitudes and activities of their elected leaders, they may not be aware of how accurately their opinions are being reflected by policymakers. A lack of congruence between public opinion and public policy could be perpetuated by public ignorance that such a situation exists. It seems likely this would be more of a problem at the state level.

A prerequisite to determining the impact of public opinion is knowledge of public opinion. This is especially a problem in state public opinion. The cost of sampling opinion in all fifty states is prohibitive. However, a technique has been developed that employs a computer program to estimate state opinions on issues from national survey data.[9] The data generated from this technique offer some insights into the role played by public opinion in shaping public policy.

The congruence between public opinion and policy in the states was simulated for 116 issues.[10] Public policy matches public opinion more closely in some states than in others. Public opinion matches policy 68 percent of the time in Idaho and New York but only 50 percent of the time in Maryland and 51 percent of the time in Vermont. The impact of opinion on policy does not appear to be uniform across the states. A crucial question the data cannot answer is why this is so. Apparently, the process of political linkage is more effective in some states than it is in others.

Using the same data, one can examine the impact of public opinion on policy for five important issues—legal lotteries, capital punishment, right-to-work laws, antidiscrimination laws, and gun controls.[11] Overall, policy conforms to opinion only 58 percent of the time. That is not very impressive—by chance, opinion and policy should match each other 50 percent of the time. However, dramatic differences emerge among policy areas. At one extreme, almost a perfect match exists between opinion and antidiscrimination (public accommodations) policy while, at the other extreme, opinion matches policy only 16 percent of the time in the area of gun controls. Public preferences, or demands, are converted into policy outputs more regularly in some areas than in others.

Richard Sutton examines further the responsiveness of state political systems. His examination of the data leads Sutton to conclude

> that no state is consistently representative or completely unrepresentative. While some states were responsive on more than one-half of the eleven policies, the analysis indicated that no state was responsive for all policies and considerable variation in state responsiveness could be discerned on any particular policy. For example, North Carolina which was unrepresentative on six policies was more responsive than many states with regard to right-to-work and firearms laws and motor vehicle regulations.[12]

Sutton finds greater congruence between opinion and policy in more controversial areas, such as civil rights and welfare, which have generated intense public opinion. Sutton stresses the need to differentiate among policy outputs in the study of political system responsiveness. Depending on the policy area being examined, the extent of agreement between public opinion and policy outputs is best explained by socioeconomic characteristics of the state, by politics and party activity, or by political attentiveness and electoral participation.

Weber and Shaffer assess the relative impact of public opinion, political culture, the socioeconomic environment, and political system characteristics on five policy outputs.[13] Their measures of public opinion are estimates of state opinion and strength of interest group membership. The policy outputs are similar to those examined by Munger—public accommodations laws, parochial school aid laws, right-to-work laws, teacher unionization laws, and firearms control laws. Assigning a crucial role to public opinion, the authors conclude "that preferences are generally more important determinants of state statutory output than measures of the environment and political system."[14] However, their data belie such a conclusion. General public opinion is the strongest independent variable only for public accommodations policy. For three of the policies, virtually no relationship exists between general public opinion and policy outputs. Interest group membership is the strongest independent variable only in the area of parochial school aid policy. Overall, the measures of political culture, socioeconomic environment, and political system are more strongly related to policy outputs than are the two measures of opinion.

Employing both the 50% + 1 threshold and empirically derived thresholds, Anne Hopkins examines the linkage between public opinion and public policy for nine issue areas at two points in time.[15] The derived thresholds are the percentage of favorable public opinion at which the largest number of correct predictions of public policy can be made. Hopkins finds that the derived thresholds are better predictors than is the commonly accepted threshold of 50% + 1. The derived thresholds vary in range from 32 percent to 70 percent. Thus, the level of public support necessary for adoption of a policy varies. The variation in thresholds seems to be related to the costs of decisionmaking. The greater the costs of making a decision, the more public support is required. Higher thresholds exist for the later time period than for the earlier time period.

Strong support for a link between public opinion and public policy is offered by some interesting data from the 1930s.[16] Public preferences were determined by surveys within each of the states—unlike the present, when preferences must be estimated. Public opinion is found to correlate with policy, and sometimes with change in policy, in the areas of capital punishment, a child labor amendment, and female jurors.

Public opinion is translated into policy principally through the mediating efforts of legislators. This means that state legislators must assume a large share of the responsibility for the responsiveness of state political systems. If opinion is to be reflected in policy outputs, state legislators must either share the same policy attitudes as their constituents and vote accordingly, or correctly perceive constituency attitudes and cast votes in accordance with those perceptions.

Evidence exists to support the notion that legislators often vote their own attitudes. In a study of Texas legislators' votes on three categories of issues—humanitarianism and two clusters of tax issues— the strongest linkage for legislators in both houses and for all issue areas was from the legislators' attitudes to the roll-call vote.[17] In fact, negative correlations were found between legislators' perceptions of constituency attitudes and roll-call votes in all three areas. These findings led the author to conclude:

> The overall impression one gets from the data is that there is little connection between the policy activity of the typical Texas legislator and the policy attitudes of his constituency through the mechanism of responsiveness. When the representative does not reflect his perceptions of his constituency's attitudes in his roll-call behavior, responsiveness cannot occur, and the question of misperception is moot.[18]

Legislators apparently are likely to vote their own attitudes, which might not conform to constituency attitudes.

In addition to voting their own attitudes, legislators can also vote their perceptions of constituency attitudes. Votes based on perceptions of constituency attitudes will accurately represent the policy desires of constituents only if such perceptions are accurate. Studies examining the ability of state legislators to perceive the attitudes of their constituents produce mixed results.

Florida legislators did a very good job of predicting how their constituents would vote on two of three referenda.[19] The referenda concerned school busing, school prayer, and equal educational opportunities for all students. Only on the educational issue were the individual predictions significantly off the mark. The median error in prediction was 6 percent on the busing issue, 9 percent on the question of school prayer, and 12 percent on the equal education vote.

Iowa legislators were asked to predict how their constituents would vote on four constitutional amendments.[20] Their predictions were good for two of the issues and poor for the other two. The legislators were accurate 92 percent of the time on the issue of home rule and 82 percent of the time on the issue of reapportionment. On the other hand, they were accurate only 64 percent of the time on the question of the item veto and only 59 percent of the time on the issue of annual sessions. Only one-third of the legislators were able to predict correctly how their constituents would vote on all four issues.

The authors of the study were also able to compare the legislators' roll-call votes on the constitutional issues with their perceptions of constituency attitudes.[21] Roll-call votes corresponded with perceived constituency attitudes 82 percent of the time. The votes were consistent with actual constituency opinion 71 percent of the time. The authors concluded that perceptions of constituency opinions do influence legislators' roll-call votes.

Three other studies offer data relating to the congruence between constituency opinion and legislators' roll-call votes. Eighty-five percent of Texas legislators voted in congruence with their constituents on the issue of liquor-by-the-drink, while only 45 percent reflected constituency attitudes on the issue of annual legislative sessions.[22] Montana legislators, especially state senators and Republican legislators, were found frequently to cast roll-call votes that differed significantly from constituency opinion in the area of environmental legislation.[23]

James Kuklinski measured the correlation between constituency liberalism as measured by referenda and initiative votes and the liberalism of California state legislators as measured by roll-call votes.[24] The overall agreement is low for both houses for the four-year period of the study. Kuklinski discovered that responsiveness increases with the proximity of elections. Senators, who serve four-year terms, are more responsive in those years in which they face reelection. Assemblymen, who serve two-year terms, do not show any variation in their level of responsiveness.

Legislators gauge constituency opinion accurately on some issues, less accurately on others. The previously discussed studies suggest that legislators are best able to predict opinion for the more salient issues of home rule, reapportionment, liquor-by-the-drink, and school busing. On issues of less concern to their constituents, legislators have more difficulty in assessing district attitudes. The policy desires of citizens apparently are more likely to be realized on issues of greater controversy: that is of great significance for a political system.

To this point, the relationship between public opinion and policy outputs has been treated as though opinion influenced policy. But it is also possible that policy outputs influence public opinion. Citizens' attitudes about certain policies are likely to be altered after outputs are produced by the political system and the impacts of the policies are apparent. Shaffer and Weber suggest that the relationship between opinion and policy is one of dynamic interaction.[25] Change in the level of congruence between opinion and policy could be due to a change in either public opinion or policy.

> At another point in time, a new balance between opinion and policy may be struck. The degree of policy responsiveness, as we have labeled this relationship, may be the same as in the previous point in time and space, or it may be considerably greater or smaller. Such a change could be generated either by an alteration in public policy or by a shift in public opinion. The linkage mechanisms, of course, would be an integral part of the new balance.[26]

Support for the notion that policy can influence public opinion exists among their data.

> In the first place, for capital punishment and parochial school aid legislation, our analysis indicates that a change in opinion was one of the principal determinants of increased nondirectional and directional responsiveness. For these two areas of state regulation, there was little or no change at all in policy; instead, greater responsiveness occurred when the citizenry changed its opinion to conform with existing public policy.[27]

In the policy areas of firearms control, police and teacher unionization, and right-to-work legislation, a different pattern exists between opinion and policy. In these areas, substantial increases in opinion support outstripped changes in policy outputs. The result was to reduce the congruence between public opinion and policy.

Shaffer and Weber's research implies that the relationship between public opinion and policy outputs is neither simple nor unidirectional.

At present, it is not possible to state that public opinion always influences public policy. On the other hand, it seems clear that at least sometimes, and at least on some issues, the public will does prevail.

FEDERAL AID

As was discussed earlier in this chapter, the amount of interstate variation in governmental expenditures accounted for by the three socioeconomic variables employed by Fabricant and other economists has decreased. The explanation offered was the increase in federal grants-in-aid. Federal aid to state and local governments has increased dramatically during the past three decades. Total federal aid to state and local governments went from approximately $2 billion a year in fiscal 1950 to approximately $87 billion a year in fiscal 1982. Federal aid now accounts for one-fifth of state government revenues. Of concern here is the impact of federal aid on state policy outputs.

Ernest Kurnow offers some of the earliest evidence of an association between federal aid and policy outputs.[28] He finds that a 10 percent increase in per capita federal aid produces a 2.6 percent increase in per capita state and local governmental expenditures.

Sacks and Harris further document the impact of federal aid on state policy, especially welfare and highway policies.[29] Introducing federal aid into their regression equation increases the amount of explained variance from 37 percent to 83 percent for highway policies and from 11 percent to 83 percent for welfare policies (see Table 3.1). For total direct general expenditures, the amount of variance explained is increased from 53 percent to 81 percent. State aid is also included among their variables and is found to be especially important in local school and health-hospital policies. When the influence of other variables is controlled for, federal aid has the strongest association with welfare and highway policies. Sacks and Harris conclude that it is impossible to understand state and local governmental expenditures without taking into account the activity of the federal government.

A slightly different perspective on the impact of federal aid is offered by Bahl and Saunders.[30] They examine the influence of changes in the level of federal aid on changes in the level of state and local governmental expenditures. They discover "that change in per capita federal grants to states is the only factor which significantly affects changes in state and local per capita spending, when data for all 48 states are included in a five variable correlation model."[31] In fact, while a model employing all five variables explains approximately 46 percent of the interstate variation, a simple correlation

TABLE 3.1. Coefficients of Multiple Determinations (R^2) for Regressions of Per Capita General Expenditures on Three Basic Factors and with State Aid and Federal Aid Added, 1960

Expenditure Category	Three Basic Factors (Equation A)	State Aid Added (Equation B)	Federal Aid Added (Equation C)	Federal and State Aid Added (Equation D)
Total direct general	.532	.667	.813	.869
Highways	.370	.375	.834	.856
Public welfare	.114	.181	.830	.858
Local schools	.604	.721	N.C.*	N.C.*
Health and hospitals	.435	.547	.472	.557
Not specifically aided and all other	.577	.602	.627	.645

*N.C. = Not computed.

Source: Seymour Sacks and Robert Harris, "The Determinants of State and Local Government Expenditures and Intergovernmental Flows of Funds," *National Tax Journal* 17 (March 1964): 81.

with federal aid explains 39 percent of the variation. However, with the exception of expenditures for highways and institutions of higher learning, their model explains much less of the variation in spending in particular functional areas. In the two functional areas where the model does account for a significant part of the variation, federal aid is the crucial variable. When fifteen high income–high density states are isolated for examination, the impact of federal aid is practically nil. When all forty-eight states are examined, the federal aid variable explains 34 percent of the variation, while when the fifteen states are examined separately the variable explains only .57 percent of the variation.

Similar findings resulted in another study measuring the effect of change in federal aid on changes in state expenditures.[32] The influence was greatest on welfare spending, but it also existed in total expenditures and highway expenditures.

Evidence has also been produced to support the proposition that growth in federal payments to state and local governments accounts for a major portion of the enlargements of both the scope and quality of state and local government services.[33]

Strouse and Jones contend that not only is federal aid an important variable in state policy research, but it also has become increasingly important over time.[34] They find that this pattern holds even when socioeconomic and political variables are controlled for. They examined the impact of federal aid on expenditures for highways, education, and welfare between 1940 and 1968.

Dye presents recent data that substantiates many of the earlier works.[35] He demonstrates that federal aid can increase significantly the amount of variation explained in state and local spending (see Table 3.2). As was noted earlier, the most dramatic impact is on welfare and highway spending. In 1980, the introduction of the federal aid variable increases the amount of variance explained in total expenditures from 41 percent to 89 percent, in welfare from 25 percent to 56 percent, and in highways from 32 percent to 68 percent.

Federal aid apparently can influence state and local governmental expenditures, at least in such areas as welfare and highways.[36] Federal grant-in-aid programs apparently also can influence how rapidly states adopt particular policies and when they adopt them.

In a study of innovation among the states, Virginia Gray suggests that patterns of diffusion will vary with the degree of federal intervention.[37] She cites the example of state merit systems for employees working in welfare agencies. Before the passage of the Social Security Act, only nine states had such plans, but after the passage of the act thirty-two states adopted a merit system governing such state employees. Subsequently, the remaining seven states adopted a merit plan. This implies that federal involvement in an area can affect state policy actions.

Another study examined fifty-seven policies in an attempt to determine the influence of federal incentives on the diffusion rate of innovative policies among the states.[38] It was discovered that federally affected policies diffused, on the average, in about thirty years while state preserve policies needed an average of slightly over fifty years to diffuse. Those policies with positive fiscal incentives diffused faster than federally affected policies without such incentives. Diffusion rates differed little by functional area. One must be cautious in making inferences from the data, however. As Welch and Thompson note, "In all, our predictions explain only between one-quarter and one-third of the variation in diffusion rates, and far less

TABLE 3.2. The Linkages between Environmental Resource, Federal Aid, and State-Local Spending

	Percentage of State-Local Spending Determined by						
State-Local Expenditures	Economic Development[a]					Economic Development Plus Federal Aid[b]	
	1942	1957	1960	1970	1980	1970	1980
Total expenditures	72	53	53	62	41	72	89
Education	59	62	60	52	36	67	71
Highways	29	34	37	50	32	86	68
Public welfare	45	14	11	17	25	48	56
Health and hospitals	72	46	44	37	6	38	31
Police	81	74	79	69	52	70	63

Note: Figures are coefficients of multiple determination (R^2) for 48 states in 1942, 1957, and 1960, and 50 states in 1970 and 1980.

[a]Economic development is defined as per capita income, population density, and percentage urbanization.

[b]Three economic development variables plus per capita federal aid.

Source: Thomas R. Dye, *Understanding Public Policy*, 4th ed. (Englewood Cliffs, N.J.: Prentice-Hall, 1984), p. 301. Figures for 1942, 1957, and 1960 from Seymour Sacks and Robert Harris, "The Determinants of State and Local Government Expenditures and Intergovernmental Flow of Funds," *National TAX Journal* 17 (March 1964): 79–85. Figures for 1970 and 1980 calculated by Thomas R. Dye.

(between three and 18 percent) when the R^2 is corrected for sample size."[39]

For the most part, analysts of state policy view the fifty states as separate political systems. Certainly the mainstream model manifests such an assumption. However, given the evidence of the crucial role played by the national government in shaping state policies, perhaps such a perspective is not appropriate. Perhaps, rather than being separate political systems, the states are merely constituent parts of a larger, national political system. Even Dye hints that such a conceptualization might be more accurate, observing that it is difficult to treat the fifty American states as separate political systems, even from an analytic standpoint.

The way in which the states respond to economic development inputs depends in considerable measure on the posture of the federal government. Occasionally the effect of federal policy is to offset the impact of levels of economic development on state policy outcomes. A notable example of this effect occurs in per capita welfare expenditures. In other areas federal policy appears to accentuate policy differences among the states. For example, federal highway aid to rural states strengthens rural-urban differences in per capita highway expenditures. Thus, state political systems are conditioned by their place in the American federal system.[40]

This position is argued more forcefully by Douglas Rose.[41] He contends that social, economic, and representational differences are greater among the states than are policy differences. For example, for the 116 policy issues examined by Munger, on the average, 83 percent of the states had the same basic law. This leads Rose to contend that the principal objective of state policy analysis should be to explain the similarities among state policies. He attributes similarities in state policies to the influence of national policies. In a number of key policy areas, national legislation has severely restricted the options available to state policymakers. As Rose writes, "the broad trend is for national patterns to override state differences in policy making and the consequence is increasing similarity among states in the effects of policy."[42]

Thus, for Rose, to treat states as the units of analysis presents conceptual problems. A meaningful understanding of state policies can only be obtained by considering national, and local, influences on the state policymaking process. National legislation often sets boundaries within which state policymakers must operate, and local government officials are often crucial in the implementation of policies. Rose believes that "states are not political systems, though they are parts of a political system."[43]

State policies are not, therefore, the "outputs" of a state system with state "inputs." Rather, state policies are mainly the product of national policy trends, between-state communications and imitations, local within-state interests, and some state level political and socioeconomic considerations.[44]

Hofferbert maintains that state policies have become increasingly similar over the years.[45] In fact, the states that had spent at the lowest levels and collected the fewest taxes have increased those activities at a faster rate than states at higher levels of spending and taxing. Hofferbert attributes part of this trend to the impact of federal aid. For example, the one policy area he examines that is not characterized by increasing similarity is general assistance. This is the only welfare program supported exclusively by state funds. However, he cautions against attributing too much influence to the role of the national government.

Hofferbert's argument is amplified in an article written with Ira Sharkansky.[46] Discussing the trend identified earlier by Hofferbert, they contend that a process of "nationalization" is taking place in the United States. Table 3.3 presents their data showing that policy variation among the states is declining. In part, they suggest, this is due to grants-in-aid, especially those with variable matching formulas (a formula that requires poorer states to put up fewer matching dollars than wealthier states). Since few grants contain such formulas—only 7 out of 442 categorical grants in fiscal 1975—this could hardly account for the trend. They state that there is no definitive explanation for the increasing policy similarity among the states.

TABLE 3.3. Coefficients of Relative Variation in Expenditures by State and Local Governments for Selected Policies: 1890–1962

Year	Total State & Local	Education	Highways	Health & Hospitals	Police	Welfare
1890	54.69	48.43	83.66	141.06	106.82	81.74
1902	51.07	52.25	53.95	55.86	94.46	68.40
1913	49.45	62.58	48.63	75.76	59.04	59.88
1930	34.54	42.13	56.82	109.09	101.19	65.30
1947	29.21	26.24	41.75	47.13	52.94	55.64
1957	21.27	21.47	33.53	33.39	36.85	40.86
1962	19.21	21.50	35.16	30.84	35.28	35.84

Source: Richard I. Hofferbert and Ira Sharkansky, "The Nationalization of State Politics," in State and Urban Politics: Readings in Comparative Public Policy, ed. Richard I. Hofferbert and Ira Sharkansky (Boston: Little, Brown, 1971), p. 472.

What seems most plausible to them is that states emulate policies adopted by other states.

A direct test of the nationalization process fails to confirm its existence.[47] Examined were states' per capita expenditures for education, health, highways, and welfare between 1958 and 1974. Measures of relative and absolute variation were used to see if the trend identified by Hofferbert continued through the 1970s. The four policy areas maintained the same relative position during the years examined. Moreover, the amount of absolute variation actually increased. The author concludes that "there is little evidence to support a 'nationalization' thesis."[48]

A recent attempt to update the research on the nationalization question finds that the variation among the states is decreasing at different rates.[49] State expenditure policies display less variation in 1980 than they did in 1940, but the rate of homogenization has slowed down, in some cases almost completely, for most policies. The period of rapid homogenization of policy apparently was from 1940 to 1960. However, the reduction of variation among the states for socioeconomic and political characteristics continues at a rapid rate. The 1970s and 1980s have continued to see a rapid reduction in the amount of relative variation in a number of such characteristics. Presently, rates of relative variation for state policies are twice as great as are those for socioeconomic and political characteristics.

A dramatic regional difference still remains. Southern states remain significantly different from the rest of the nation on most characteristics. Differences between southern states and other states for expenditure policies continue to be significant or have become significant. The same pattern exists for most of the socioeconomic and political characteristics. Interestingly, while all of the states are becoming increasingly similar over time, and while southern states vary less from the rest of the states than previously, southern states remain unique.

Resolution lies in the fact that nonsouthern states have become extremely homogeneous over time. Even though southern mean values have become closer to those for the fifty states over all variables, the southern states have remained or become an even more outlying group relative to the other states. For all policy variables and most socioeconomic and political variables, the relative distance between southern and nonsouthern states has increased even though the absolute distance has decreased. As a result, the southern states have continued to be significantly different from the rest of the country on some variables, and have become significantly different on others.[50]

Enough empirical evidence has been produced to sustain the proposition that state policy outputs are not always exclusively attributable to forces operating within the states. The influence of the national government seems to vary with the policy area, being greatest in such areas as welfare and highways.

REGIONALISM

Sharkansky finds that regionalism is significantly correlated with policy outputs even when controlling for economic characteristics of states.[51] Regionalism has also been associated with policy innovation among the states.[52] It has been reported that "a portion of the variance in American state innovation adoption rates appears to be associated with regional proximity, even after the impact of similar economic and political structures is controlled for."[53]

Region apparently has a differential impact on policy. It is the most important factor in explaining welfare and education policy, after controlling for the effects of economic and political influences.[54] Interestingly, the only regional distinction of importance was whether or not a state was located in the South. Southern regional location accounted for over half of the variation among the states. Southern states tended to spend less in these policy areas than did nonsouthern states. In the case of highway and natural resource policy, region accounts for virtually none of the variation among the states. Region apparently does have an impact on policy, but that impact would appear to vary by policy area.

POLITICAL CULTURE

Related to regionalism is the concept of political culture. Probably the most influential work on political cultures in the United States is that by Daniel Elazar.[55] On the basis of impressionistic evidence, Elazar identifies three political cultures in the American states: moralistic, individualistic, and traditionalistic. Politics in the moralistic culture involves a search for the good society. Citizens are concerned with issues and political participation is encouraged. Participation should be for the sake of the commonwealth; likewise, governmental intervention is welcomed for the benefit of the commonwealth. The moralistic culture values a large, professional, well-paid bureaucracy. The moralistic culture also welcomes new programs that will benefit the commonwealth.

In the individualistic political culture, there is an emphasis on the democratic order as a marketplace. Participation can be used as a means of improving one's social and economic position. Corruption is tolerated by citizens in the individualistic culture. Little value is assigned to a concern with issues. Limited governmental intervention is favored. Bureaucracy is viewed with ambivalence by the citizens. On the one hand, it is not congruent with the system of favors that characterizes this culture. On the other hand, it is an organization that can be used by public officials to further their own interests. New programs will be initiated only when the public demand for such programs is overwhelming.

The traditionalistic political culture has roots in a precommercial order characterized by hierarchical social relationships and a paternalistic view of politics. Participation is not expected to be widespread—it is reserved for those of elite status. Governmental intervention is acceptable only to the extent that it maintains the status quo. A professional bureaucracy is viewed with suspicion, because it tends to undermine the power of the dominant groups. Where it exists, it exercises only minimal functions under the control of members of the power structure. New programs will be welcomed only if they are required to help maintain the status quo.

While the relationship between political culture and public policy was not a primary concern of Elazar's, he reports that states with a moralistic culture are more likely to adopt innovative programs and antidiscrimination laws.[56]

A much more extensive examination of the relationship between political culture and policy is conducted by Sharkansky.[57] He constructs a scale of political culture from the within-state designations made by Elazar. The scale conceptualizes political culture as a continuum running from moralistic through individualistic to traditionalistic. He then correlates this scale with sixteen measures of policy outputs. Nine of the measures have statistically significant simple correlations with the scale of political culture. All of the relationships fit with Elazar's notions about the respective cultures. States that fall more toward the traditionalistic end of the scale have lower scores on measures of tax effort, governmental spending, and public services. All but one of the correlations remains statistically significant even after income and urbanism are controlled for. Finally, a majority remain significant statistically when region is controlled for.

Here is evidence that political culture is related to policy outputs. But some notes of caution are in order. The scale of political culture is most strongly correlated with measures of political participation—voter turnout and the restrictiveness of suffrage regulations. Sharkansky suggests that culture may have its most direct effects on popular behavior, as evidenced by the strong relationship with the measures of participation. The association with policy may be more indirect. Sharkansky concludes by stating that "Elazar's designations for the political cultures of each state—and sub-areas within the states—are of questionable reliability. They are also limited in the number of traits of each political culture that they assess. These findings are more suggestive than definitive."[58]

Charles Johnson develops indices based on religious affiliation to classify states in Elazar's categories.[59] These categories are then related to certain policy outputs. Welfare and highway expenditures are higher in states with moralistic and individualistic cultures. Governmental innovation also tends to be higher in states with these two political cultures. Most of the relationships reported by Johnson hold up after economic variables are controlled for.

Leonard Ritt uses Sharkansky's scale of political culture to examine the relationship between political culture and political reform.[60] Ritt hypothesizes that moralistic cultures will be most conducive to reform and traditionalistic cultures will be most hostile to reform. His findings generally confirm his hypothesis. States with moralistic cultures have more reformed legislatures and judiciaries and are more receptive to program innovation. The relationships hold up when controls are employed for income and education.

State policies in the areas of local tax limitations and state aid to local governments have been found to be consistent and related to variations among the states' populations' dispositions to support governmental expenditure.[61] The variation in liberal attitudes is partly a reflection of cultural differences as measured by Sharkansky's scale. Political culture is one of the strongest variables in Shaffer and Weber's study. Culture is associated with general responsiveness to public opinion as well as responsiveness in a conservative or liberal direction.[62]

Apparently, public policies do vary among the states according to variations in political culture. The key, unanswered question is asked by Lowery and Sigelman: "Why do moralistic, individualistic, and traditionalistic cultures differ from one another in the policies their governments pursue?"[63] Lowery and Sigelman contend that two assumptions are made to account for the link between culture and policy. The first is that citizens in states with different cultures hold differing attitudes about such things as mass participation and the role of government, which is reflected in policies. The second assumption is that mass attitudes are the crucial factor in the determination of public policies. The authors use data from the Center for Political Studies 1978 American National Election Study to ascertain whether distinctive attitudes about mass participation and the desirable scope of government are associated with Elazar's three political cultures. For each respondent, the authors use both the dominant culture of the state in which the respondent currently resides and the dominant political culture of the state in which he or she grew up. The latter is used because of Americans' high level of mobility.

Their results provide only limited support for Elazar's observations. As could be expected, current residents of states with a predominantly moralistic culture are more politically efficacious, see government as being more responsive, and have a higher sense of citizen duty than do residents of traditionalistic cultures. Both present and past residents of moralistic states also view governmental activity less negatively than do residents of traditionalistic states. But this relationship is not statistically significant. Residents of predominantly individualistic states, as suggested by Elazar, hold attitudes that are midway between those of residents of moralistic and traditionalistic states. Both present and past residents of individualistic states are more likely than are residents of traditionalistic states to favor governmental action to deal with social problems.

While these attitudes comport with Elazar's observations, there are other instances where no differences emerge among the cultures, and two instances where significant relationships are discovered that run counter to Elazar's expectations. When the culture associated with the current place of residence is employed, only seven of twelve predictions based on Elazar's designations are confirmed by the data; when the culture associated with the formative years is used, only five of twelve predictions attain statistical significance. Lowery and Sigelman conclude that "to judge by the criterion of statistical significance, then, the performance of the political culture variables as predictors of attitudes related to political participation and the desired scope of government activity is modest at best."[64] In a related work, Schlitz and Rainey arrive at conclusions that echo the sentiments of Lowery and Sigelman.[65]

According to Lowery and Sigelman, mass political attitudes apparently cannot account for the policy differences that have been uncovered across political cultures. They suggest two alternative factors that might provide the link between political culture and public policy: elite cultures and cultural lag. Either or both of these factors might be the key. Even in the absence of mass cultural differences, political elites might hold divergent attitudes tied to cultural variations that influence policy. After all, elites do exercise the greatest influence on policy. Cultural lag allows for the possibility that attitudes from an earlier period may continue to exert influence: "The growing homogenization of American politics may well have obliterated major culturally defined differences in outlooks, but the operation of key political institutions may continue to reflect the attitudes that prevailed in an earlier era."[66]

Support for the proposition that intercultural differences exist among elites is offered by Welch and Peters in several studies. The elite group examined was a sample of state senators in twenty-four randomly selected states. Culture was measured by Sharkansky's scale. Initially, differences were examined among the elites in attitudes toward political corruption.[67] Elites in states with a moralistic political culture were less likely to tolerate corrupt behavior and to believe that it occurred in their legislatures than were elites in states with a traditionalistic or individualistic culture. Welch and Peters then expanded their investigation to include attitudes on economic-welfare policy, the new social issues, and self-designated liberalism as well as political corruption.[68] They found that legislators from states with a moralistic political culture were most likely to favor social change, to support governmental intervention on economic welfare issues, to be self-declared liberals, and to feel that political corruption was a significant problem. Legislators in states with a traditionalistic culture were the most conservative and were the least likely to believe corruption to be a problem. Legislators from states with an individualistic culture held intermediate positions in all four areas.

Welch and Peters report that political culture is also related to liberalism on the economic-welfare and social-issues dimensions.[69] Legislators from states with a traditionalistic culture tended to be more conservative on both dimensions than legislators from states with either moralistic or individualistic cultures.

The Elazar-Sharkansky index of political culture is strongly related to a factor labeled "general policy liberalism" (GPL).[70] The GPL factor is composed of six expenditure and nonexpenditure variables. States with a liberal, active, moralistic political culture score higher on the GPL factor. Specifically, states displaying more policy liberalism tend to be nonsouthern coastal and Great Lakes states plus Colorado, those with greater population diversity, and those with higher rates of population loss. Southern, southwestern, and border states score lower on the GPL factor, as do states with less population diversity and those with higher rates of population gain. There is thus a distinction between snowbelt and sunbelt states. Klingman and Lammers suggest that these patterns pose interesting questions about the future.

Fundamental questions regarding future policy responses thus emerge. The "snowbelt" states have in the past enjoyed relatively high levels of wealth and revenue to help sustain their propensity for more expansive use of the public sector. Given the extent of their recent economic decline, as well as population loss, their future levels of public policy effort are clearly in doubt. To what extent will the social, cultural, and political forces underlying their past commitments be sufficient to sustain similar actions in the face of economic and fiscal austerity? Conversely, one wonders whether the more conservative elements in the social and political culture of the "sunbelt" states will continue to constrain the pressures for an expanding public sector which typically arise from increasing economic activity and potential government revenue, and from the increasingly complex problems generated by growth.[71]

In contrast to Elazar's impressionistic formulation of political cultures, Norman Luttbeg offers four empirically derived cultures.[72] Luttbeg's cultures are derived from factor analyzing 118 variables measuring the political process, economic development, and public policy. States share a common culture because they have a large number of common characteristics. The four cultures identified are Industrial, Southern, Sparsely Populated, and Frontier.

The states in each culture display a tendency to cluster together geographically. The Industrial states are concentrated on the east and west coasts and in the Great Lakes area. The Sparsely Populated states are found in the Great Plains and Rocky Mountain regions, plus the states of Vermont and New Hampshire. The Southern states are found in the South and Southwest. The Frontier states are Nevada, Alaska, and Hawaii.

Policy differences exist among the four cultures. The Industrialized states have fewer citizens receiving welfare and disability payments, and these states assume a larger portion of the costs of school and highway programs. The Southern states receive a large percentage of their public assistance and welfare expenditures from the federal government, but they assume responsibility for highway expenditures and provide a large portion of state and local welfare expenditures. These states also make broad use of income and sales taxes. The Sparsely Populated states spend a high percentage of money on highways and receive a large percentage of this money from the federal government. Frontier states allocate a low percentage of state highway funds to localities, but do not discriminate against urban areas in highway expenditures. They also have few people receiving old age and general assistance. These states also obtain a high percentage of tax revenues from the income tax and a low percentage from the sales tax.

Luttbeg's classifications, on the average, account for 50 percent of the variation among the states on the 118 variables used in the analysis. By way of contrast, the Bureau of the Census's regional classification explains 22 percent of the variation and Elazar's regional classification explains 30 percent. Elazar's scheme is a considerable improvement on the Bureau of the Census's classification in accounting for policy variation.

States sharing a common culture share more than just a common geography.

Earlier we suggested that the basis of regularities rests on shared traditions, orientations, life styles, settlement patterns, resources, and problems faced. In the light of this classification, it seems improbable that physical resources and problems derived from climate and geography have a substantial impact on state political behavior. When Iowa and Idaho, Louisiana and Arizona, and Minnesota and California share behavior, geography would seem unimportant. Rather, shared values, social bases, traditions, and problems faced would seem to be the sources of regularity. It would seem that man rather than the land achieves the similarities of actions noted.[73]

THE INFLUENCE OF THE ENVIRONMENT ON POLICY OVER TIME

The evidence presented in this chapter documents that, to some extent at least, policy outputs are influenced by environmental circumstances. Has the relationship between the environment and policy outputs been altered over time? The answer appears to be yes. As the data in Table 3.2 portrayed, the relationship between the socioeconomic environment and policy outputs has been reduced while the impact of federal aid has increased. This points out both the variable impact of the environment on policy and the complex nature of the linkage abetween the environment and policy outputs.

There is less variation among the states in social and economic conditions than in the past (see Table 3.4). The states are becoming more similar in terms of income, education, urbanization, and industrialization. Moreover, states that traditionally have been poorer and less industrialized are getting wealthier and more industrialized at a faster rate than those states that have been the leaders in these areas.

Concomitant with increasing environmental similarity among the states is a reduced association between economic resources and policy outputs (see Table 3.5). This is due in part to the impact of federal aid. In part it is also due to state policymakers tapping more revenue sources. In 1984, forty-five states had a general sales tax, forty-five had a corporate income tax, and forty had a personal income tax. State lotteries are now employed in a growing number of states. Prior to the 1984 election, seventeen states had lotteries. The 1984 election saw voters in four additional states approve lottery referenda.

This reduced dependence on economic conditions affords state policymakers the opportunity to provide services beyond what might be expected, given their level of economic resources. Hofferbert suggests that policymakers now have the potential for greater choice in policymaking.[74] This happens because once available resources en-

TABLE 3.4. Coefficients of Relative Variation in Selected Socio-economic Characteristics of the States: 1890–1960

Year	% Population Employed in Manufacturing	% Population Urban	% Population Illiterate	Per Capita Personal Income
1890	NA	68	89	NA
1900	86	68	89	NA
1910	92	57	84	NA
1920	75	51	84	NA
1930	72	43	84	36
1940	74	39	NA	37
1950	66	29	65	23
1960	52	24	61	21
1970	NA	22	52	21
1980	NA	21	NA	14

Source: Adapted from Richard I. Hofferbert and Ira Sharkansky, "The Nationalization of State Politics," in *State and Urban Politics: Readings in Comparative Public Policy*, ed. Richard I. Hofferbert and Ira Sharkansky (Boston: Little, Brown, 1971), p. 469, and Harvey J. Tucker, "The Nationalization of State Policy Revisited," *Western Political Quarterly* 37 (September 1984): 436.

able officials to provide a minimum level of services they are free to use their discretion.

Morehouse concurs in this assessment.

> We suspect that there may be a threshold effect at work here. Economic growth may affect policy making most clearly below a minimum "threshold" of development. The poorer the state, the less it can afford to spend on the necessary services for its citizens. The poorer the family, the less it can afford on food or shelter. This makes a great deal of sense. Grinding poverty and starvation go together for people as well as states. However, choices exist for families after a certain income is reached. No longer is life desperate and short. Money can be spent in different ways. It can be spent on education, for example, to improve one's chances in life, or it can be squandered.
>
> So it is with states. Matters other than economic development begin to have an independent effect of their own so we cannot predict a state's level of services solely on the basis of this measure. Once politics become important, economic factors become less so because the conditions themselves can be changed or controlled by the citizens.[75]

Hofferbert's data show a tendency for poorer states to devote a larger percentage of their available resources to social services than do wealthier states.

> The fact that the less advantaged states seem to commit a larger portion of their available resources to social services indicates, of course, that there are more people in need of assistance in these states. But it might make one wonder if there is not, in the minds of state policy makers throughout the country, such a thing as a "natural" level of support for the disadvantaged or for particular public activities. No matter how rich a state may be in revenue resources, public demands, technical skills, etc., the salaries of teachers in the public schools or the amount of monthly payments to the economically unfortunate are not likely to go very much beyond certain absolute levels followed in the rest of the nation.[76]

The relationship between economic conditions and policy outputs could be weakened both by poorer states providing above their means and wealthier states providing below their means.

Overall, the association between measures of the socioeconomic environment and spending by state and local governments has been weakening during the twentieth century. Among the policies listed in Table 3.2, only in the case of highway policy was the correlation between economic development and spending stronger in 1980 than

TABLE 3.5. Relationships between Per Capita State and Local Government Expenditures and Per Capita Personal Income: Coefficients of Simple Correlation

1903	.920
1932	.839
1942	.821
1957	.658
1962	.645
1964–65	.558

Source: Alan K. Campbell and Seymour Sacks, *Metropolitan America: Fiscal Patterns and Governmental Systems* (New York: Free Press, 1967), p. 57.

in 1942. For the remaining policies, the relationship was weaker, and sometimes significantly weaker. For example, the proportion of total spending explained decreased from 72 percent to 41 percent and the proportion of health and hospitals spending explained decreased from 72 percent to 6 percent. Federal aid seems to be a crucial variable in accounting for the declining significance of other environmental variables. As was described earlier, the addition of the federal aid variable increased the percentage of state and local spending explained for every policy in Table 3.2, and usually substantially.

Dye charts the association between income, education, urbanization, and industrialization and total state and local spending and spending for education and welfare from 1890 to 1976.[77] While the magnitude of all the correlations has declined, income and education have continuously been important determinants of public policy. The influence of industrialization and urbanization have been significantly reduced as all the states have become more industrialized and urbanized.

Two longitudinal studies offer exceptions to these trends. One examines the predictive ability of selected socioeconomic and political variables between 1890 and 1970.[78] Two environmental variables—party competition and popular participation—and two political variables—Hofferbert's industrialization and affluence factors—are employed. The policy measures are four dimensions each of state spending and state-local spending: total spending, highway expenditures per capita, education expenditures per capita, and welfare expenditures per capita. The impact of federal aid is also assessed. The findings indicate that socioeconomic development continues to be strongly associated with state and state-local spending. As the authors conclude, "Socioeconomic development, as measured by level of industrialization and affluence, has been the most important determinant of spending levels in the American states in this period, but in general has been decreasing in explanatory power."[79]

The impact of federal aid is judged to be minimal. The data offer no support for the notion that federal aid has become a crucial determinant of state spending.

The second study covers the years 1958 to 1977 and examines the relationship between personal income and educational expenditures, AFDC expenditures, and tax revenues.[80] The relationships between income and tax revenues and welfare expenditures are persistent and stable over time, and the relationship between income and educational expenditures has actually increased over time. In addition, certain states tended to be consistent deviants in either spending above or below expected levels based on their income levels.

These studies suggest that the relationship between the environment and policy outputs has not been lessened during this century.

SUMMARY

Beginning with the writings of several economists, a linkage has been established between the environment and policy outputs. The most frequently established relationship is between economic development and policy. Policy is conceptualized as being, in large part, a response by policymakers to environmental conditions. Such environmental conditions as income, education, urbanization, and industrialization are seen as setting boundaries within which policymakers must operate.

Public opinion shapes demands that are directed toward policymakers. It is assumed that in a democracy policymakers will respond to public opinion. Public policy is supposed to reflect public attitudes. The evidence presented in this chapter suggests that this often is not the case. The overall congruence between opinion and policy in the American states is only slightly better than what could be expected by chance. However, noticeable differences exist among policy areas. Civil rights is an example of a policy area where public opinion exerts considerable influence while gun control is an example of an area where the public will seldom prevails. Public opinion can influence policy, but public opinion does not always restrict policymakers.

State legislators are the conduits through which public opinion travels until it emerges as policy. However, legislators often vote their own attitudes in opposition to constituency attitudes and often misperceive constituency attitudes on issues. What is most encouraging, however, is that legislators' perceptions seem to be most accurate on the most volatile issues. It is on issues of less concern to constituents that lawmakers most often misread voters' opinions.

Federal aid has become an increasingly important determinant of state policy. Statistically, federal aid increases the amount of variance explained by economic development. Grants-in-aid also influence the adoption of programs by states. States are more likely to adopt a program if the national government is involved in an area; states are even more likely to adopt if the national government provides positive financial incentives. Federal aid has been especially important in such areas as welfare and highways.

Variation in policy outputs among the states has been declining during this century. The influence of grants-in-aid is undoubtedly partially responsible. But apparently emulation is also a factor. States will copy programs that have been successful in other states. At least one political scientist, Douglas Rose, contends that what is most striking about the states today is the similarity of policies. This has led Rose, and also Dye, to suggest that perhaps states should not be considered separate political systems. National legislation may be more important than state-level inputs in determining policy outputs in the American states.

Environmental differences among the states have also been declining since the end of the last century. States are becoming more similar on such characteristics as income, education, urbanization, and industrialization. Associated with this is a reduced correlation between measures of the socioeconomic environment and policy outputs. Income and education have been associated with policy more persistently than have urbanization and industrialization. The growing importance of federal aid probably helps to explain the reduced relationship between policy and the socioeconomic variables. Because the socioeconomic environment now exerts less control over policymakers, they probably have greater latitude in setting policy.

We have examined how different aspects of the environment influence policy. Certainly, policy is not made in a political, social, and economic vacuum. Demands for policy, and resources available to policymakers, help to determine the nature and extent of state policies. But policy does not just happen—it must be adopted and implemented by occupants of the political system. Next, we turn our attention to the political system and its influence on state policy.

NOTES

1. Solomon Fabricant, *The Trend of Government Activity in the United States Since 1900* (New York: National Bureau of Economic Research, 1952), pp. 12–39.

2. Glenn W. Fisher, "Determinants of State and Local Government Expenditures: A Preliminary Analysis," *National Tax Journal* 14 (December 1961): 349–55.

3. Seymour Sacks and Robert Harris, "The Determinants of State and Local Government Expenditures and Intergovernmental Flows of Funds," *National Tax Journal* 17 (March 1964): 75–85.

4. Glenn W. Fisher, "Interstate Variation in State and Local Government Expenditures," *National Tax Journal* 17 (March 1964): 57–74.

5. Thomas R. Dye, *Understanding Public Policy*, 5th ed. (Englewood Cliffs, N.J.: Prentice-Hall, 1984), p. 301.

6. Ira Sharkansky, "Economic Theories of Public Policy: Resource-Policy and Need-Policy Linkages Between Income and Welfare Benefits," *Midwest Journal of Political Science* 15 (November 1971): 722–40.

7. Ibid., p. 725.

8. Ibid.

9. A description of the methodology can be found in Ronald E. Weber, *Public Policy Preferences in the States* (Bloomington: Indiana University Institute of Public Administration, 1971).

10. Frank J. Munger, "Opinions, Elections, Parties, and Policies: A Cross-State Analysis," paper presented at the Annual Meeting of the American Political Science Association, New York, 1969, p. 18, as adapted and presented by George C. Edwards III and Ira Sharkansky, *The Policy Predicament: Making and Implementing Public Policy* (San Francisco: Freeman, 1978), p. 22.

11. Frank J. Munger, "Opinions, Elections, Parties, and Policies: A Cross-State Analysis," paper delivered at Annual Meeting of the American Political Science Association, New York, 1969, as presented in Thomas R. Dye, *Politics in States and Communities*, 2nd ed. (Englewood Cliffs: Prentice-Hall, 1973), p. 82.

12. Richard L. Sutton, "The States and the People: Measuring and Accounting for 'State Representativeness,'" *Polity* 5 (Summer 1973): pp. 475.

13. Ronald E. Weber and William R. Shaffer, "Public Opinion and American State Policy-Making," *Midwest Journal of Political Science* 16 (November 1972): 683–99.

14. Ibid., p. 699.

15. Anne H. Hopkins, "Opinion Publics and Support for Public Policy in the American States," *American Journal of Political Science* 18 (February 1974): 167–77.

16. Robert S. Erikson, "The Relationship Between Public Opinion and State Policy: A New Look Based on Some Forgotten Data," *American Journal of Political Science* 20 (February 1976): 25–36.

17. Bryan D. Jones, "Competitiveness, Role Orientations, and Legislative Responsiveness," *Journal of Politics* 35 (November 1973): 924–47.

18. Ibid., p. 933.

19. Robert S. Erikson, Norman R. Luttbeg, and William V. Holloway, "Knowing One's District: How Legislators Predict Referendum Voting," *American Journal of Political Science* 19 (May 1975): 231–46.

20. Ronald D. Hedlund and H. Paul Friesma, "Representatives' Perceptions of Constituency Opinion," *Journal of Politics* 34 (August 1972): 730–52.

21. H. Paul Friesma and Ronald D. Hedlund, "The Reality of Representational Roles," in Luttbeg, *Public Opinion and Public Policy*, pp. 316–20.

22. William C. Adams and Paul H. Ferber, "Measuring Legislator-Constituency Congruence: Liquor, Legislators and Linkage," *Journal of Politics* 42 (February 1980): 205.

23. Jerry W. Calvert, "The Social and Ideological Bases of Support for Environmental Legislation: An Examination of Public Attitudes and Legislative Action," *Western Political Quarterly* 32 (September 1979): 327–37.

24. James H. Kuklinski, "Representativeness and Elections: A Policy Analysis," *American Political Science Review* 72 (March 1978): 165–77.

25. William R. Shaffer and Ronald E. Weber, *Policy Responsiveness in the American States* (Beverly Hills: Sage Professional Papers in Administrative and Policy Studies, Vol. 2, Series No. 03–021, 1974).

26. Ibid., pp. 54–55.

27. Ibid., p. 55.

28. Ernest Kurnow, "Determinants of State and Local Expenditures Reexamined," *National Tax Journal* 16 (September 1963): 252–55.

29. Sacks and Harris, "Determinants of State and Local Government Expenditures."

30. Roy W. Bahl, Jr., and Robert J. Saunders, "Determinants of Changes in State and Local Government Expenditures," *National Tax Journal* 18 (March 1965): 50–57.

31. Ibid., p. 51.

32. E. Terrence Jones, "Political Change and Spending Shifts in the American States," *American Politics Quarterly* 2 (April 1974): 159–78.

33. Selma J. Mushkin and Gabrielle C. Lupo, "State and Local Finance Projections: Another Dimension," *Southern Economic Journal* 33 (January 1967): 426–29.

34. James C. Strouse and Philippe Jones, "Federal Aid: The Forgotten Variable in State Policy Research," *Journal of Politics* 36 (February 1974): 200–7.

35. Dye, *Understanding Public Policy*, 5th ed., pp. 300–4.

36. For a study critical of the use of federal aid as an independent variable, see Elliott R. Morss, "Some Thoughts on the Determinants of State and Local Expenditures," *National Tax Journal* 19 (March 1966): 95–103. He charges that

inasmuch as states and localities must spend virtually all the federal aid they receive, it is not surprising to find that aid and expenditures move together, in a "statistically significant manner." Indeed, using aid to explain expenditures is analogous to using taxes to explain expenditures in the sense that both aid and taxes are sources of funds. The fact that these variables turn out to have substantial explanatory power serves as little more than verification of the quite obvious fact that government receipts and expenditures are closely related (p. 97).

37. Virginia Gray, "Innovation in the States: A Diffusion Study," *American Political Science Review* 67 (December 1973): 1180–81.

38. Susan Welch and Kay Thompson, "The Impact of Federal Incentives on State Policy Innovation," *American Journal of Political Science* 24 (November 1980): 715–29.

39. Ibid., p. 725.

40. Thomas R. Dye, *Politics, Economics, and the Public: Policy Outcomes in the American States* (Chicago: Rand McNally, 1966), p. 292.

41. Douglas D. Rose, "National and Local Forces in State Politics: The Implications of Multi-Level Policy Analysis," *American Political Science Review* 67 (December 1973): 1162–73.

42. Ibid., p. 1169.

43. Ibid., p. 1171.

44. Ibid., p. 1170.

45. Richard I. Hofferbert, "Ecological Development and Policy Change," *Midwest Journal of Political Science* 4 (November 1966): 464–83.

46. Richard I. Hofferbert and Ira Sharkansky, "The Nationalization of State Politics," in *State and Urban Politics: Readings in Comparative Public Policy*, ed. Richard I. Hofferbert and Ira Sharkansky (Boston: Little, Brown, 1971), pp. 463–74.

47. Kathleen A. Kemp, "Nationalization of the American States: A Test of the Thesis," *American Politics Quarterly* 6 (April 1978): 237–47.

48. Ibid., p. 243.

49. Harvey J. Tucker, "The Nationalization of State Policy Revisited," *Western Political Quarterly* 37 (September 1984): 435–442.

50. Ibid., pp. 439–40.

51. Ira Sharkansky, "Regionalism, Economic Status, and the Public Policies of American States," *Social Science Quarterly* 49 (June 1968): 9–26.

52. John L. Foster, "Regionalism and Innovation in the American States," *Journal of Politics* 40 (February 1978): 178–87.

53. Ibid., p. 186.

54. Marvin K. Hoffman and James E. Prather, "The Independent Effect of Region on State Governmental Expenditures," *Social Science Quarterly* 53 (June 1972): 52–65.

55. Daniel J. Elazar, *American Federalism: A View from the States*, 2nd ed. (New York: Crowell, 1972), especially Chapter 4.

56. Ibid., pp. 149–52.

57. Ira Sharkansky, "The Utility of Elazar's Political Culture," *Polity* 2 (Fall 1969): 66–83; for a criticism of Sharkansky's article, see Edward J. Clynch, "A Critique of Ira Sharkansky's 'The Utility of Elazar's Political Culture,'" *Polity* (Fall 1972): 139–41.

58. Ibid., p. 83.

59. Charles A. Johnson, "Political Culture in American States: Elazar's Formulation Examined," *American Journal of Political Science* 20 (August 1976): 491–509.

60. Leonard G. Ritt, "Political Cultures and Political Reform: A Research Note," *Publius* 4 (Winter 1974): 127–33.

61. Jeff Stonecash, "State Policies Regarding Local Resource Acquisition: Disorder, Compensatory Adjustment, or Coherent Restraint," *American Politics Quarterly* 9 (October 1981): 401–25.

62. Shaffer and Weber, *Policy Responsiveness in the American States.*

63. David Lowery and Lee Sigelman, "Political Culture and State Public Policy: The Missing Link," *Western Political Quarterly* 35 (September 1982): 376.

64. Ibid., p. 381.

65. Timothy D. Schlitz and R. Lee Rainey, "The Geographic Distribution of Elazar's Political Subcultures among the Mass Population: A Research Note," *Western Political Quarterly* 31 (September 1978): 410–15. For a critique of this article, see Robert L. Savage, "Looking for Political Subcultures: A Critique of the Rummage-Sale Approach," *Western Political Quarterly* 34 (June 1981): 331–36.

66. Lowery and Sigelman, "Political Culture and State Public Policy," p. 383.

67. John G. Peters and Susan Welch, "Politics, Corruption and Political Culture," *American Politics Quarterly* 6 (July 1978): 345–56.

68. Susan Welch and John G. Peters, "State Political Culture and the Attitudes of State Senators Toward Social, Economic Welfare, and Corruption Issues," *Publius* 10 (Spring 1980): 59–67.

69. Susan Welch and John G. Peters, "Elite Attitudes on Economic-Welfare and Social Issues," *Polity* 14 (Fall 1981): 160–77.

70. David Klingman and William W. Lammers, "The 'General Policy Liberalism' Factor in American State Politics," *American Journal of Political Science* 28 (August 1984): 598–610.

71. Ibid., p. 608.

72. Norman R. Luttbeg, "Classifying the American States: An Empirical Attempt to Identify Internal Variations," *Midwest Journal of Political Science* 15 (November 1971): 703–21.

73. Ibid., pp. 718–19.

74. Hofferbert, "Ecological Development and Policy Change," p. 481.

75. Sarah McCally Morehouse, *State Politics, Parties, and Policy* (Holt, Rinehart and Winston, 1981), pp. 28–29.

76. Hofferbert, "Ecological Development and Policy Change," p. 479.

77. Dye, *Understanding Public Policy*, 4th ed., pp. 324–26.

78. Phillip W. Roeder, *Stability and Change in the Determinants of State Expenditures* (Beverly Hills: Sage Professional Papers in American Politics, Vol. 3, Series No. 04–027, 1976).

79. Ibid., p. 30.

80. John S. Robey and Rick Jenkins, "The Economic Basis of State Policies: A Longitudinal Analysis," *Social Science Quarterly* 63 (September 1982): 566–71.

4

THE INFLUENCE
OF THE POLITICAL SYSTEM
ON POLICY OUTPUTS

Regardless of the influence of environmental factors, policies do not exist until they are formulated, adopted, and implemented by policymakers within the political system. The policymakers include representatives of interest groups, political party leaders, governors, legislators, administrators, and judges. Such individuals and others give shape to public policies. Constrained by public support and available resources, policymakers convert demands into policy outputs. This is the direct linkage between the political system and policy outputs envisioned in the mainstream model.

Political scientists have long believed that political system characteristics have consequences for policymaking. Some groups are advantaged and others are disadvantaged by specific institutional arrangements. Perhaps E. E. Schattschneider has stated it most succinctly: "All forms of political organization have a bias in favor of the exploitation of some kinds of conflict and the suppression of others because organization is the mobilization of bias. Some issues are organized into politics while others are organized out."[1] If this were so, political structures and processes could be vital determinants of policy outputs. Through the years, a number of political scientists have contended that such is the case.

Which party controls the various state offices, the degree of interparty competition within a state, how many voters report to the polls on election day and who they are, and how well a state legislature is apportioned are felt to be important because many political scientists assume that such factors have an impact on the types of policy outputs produced by a state's political system. For example, they assume that a state government controlled by Democrats will adopt policies significantly different from a government dominated by Republicans. Related to this, they believe that different policies (more liberal) will be produced in states where party competition exists than in states where one party dominates. A higher rate of voter participation is held by some to motivate policymakers to consider the demands of groups that normally might not be considered— the poor. Finally, they contend that well-apportioned legislatures should adopt policies different from those adopted by malapportioned legislatures. Specifically, urban areas of a state should be treated more equitably by a well-apportioned legislature.

Such assumptions are just that—assumptions. They must be tested empirically. This chapter will examine research that has tested these and related assumptions about the impact of the political system. The most frequently employed measures of the political system are interparty competition, the division of two-party control, voter participation, and legislative apportionment. In addition to these, we will examine the impact of legislative professionalism, several political routines, and the formal powers of the governor.

PARTY COMPETITION

Students of comparative state policy research have built upon the early works of V. O. Key,[2] Duane Lockard,[3] and John Fenton.[4] In their early works of a comparative nature, these eminent political scientists made a case for the importance of party competition. Taking these works in order of their publication, a line of development emerges.

In his classic study of southern politics, Key stresses the importance of a two-party system or a one-party system with clearly defined factions.[5] In such a system, Key believes that there is greater potential for the adoption of more liberal policies, which would benefit the have-nots. The critical element that competition provides for the political system is organization; this is especially important for the have-nots.

> It follows that the grand objective of the haves is obstruction, at least
> of the haves who take only a short-term view. Organization is not always

necessary to obstruct; it is essential, however, for the promotion of a sustained program in behalf of the have-nots, although not all party or factional organization is dedicated to that purpose. It follows, if these propositions are correct, that over the long run the have-nots lose in a disorganized politics. . . . The have–have-not match is settled in part by the fact that substantial numbers of the have-nots never get into the ring. For that reason professional politicians often have no incentive to appeal to the have-nots.[6]

Key's work deals with only one region, and a noncompetitive region at that. It is almost impossible to draw implications about the impact of party competition beyond the South. Key apparently did not intend for his findings to be extended to more competitive states.

To appraise one-party factions as instruments of popular leadership requires a comparison of the results on one-party and two-party systems. Differences in governmental action under the two systems might be attributed to dissimilarities in political organization. The problem thus phrased presupposes that one-party systems are alike, but they are not; that two-party systems are alike, but they are not. Moreover, two-party states have not been subjected to intensive analysis and the essential facts for the comparison are lacking.[7]

Lockard goes beyond Key's work by testing the proposition that competitive parties tend to be more responsive to the needs of the have-nots.[8] In states with two competitive parties, organizations exist that can express the viewpoints of the have-nots. Also, close competition means that parties ignore groups of voters at their own risk. Lockard contends that tax laws and expenditures for public services are more in the interest of the have-nots in the three competitive states in his study than in the three one-party states. Moreover, two-party competition helps to mitigate the conservative influence of malapportionment.

Lockard notes, in the case of expenditures for the less fortunate, that party competition might not be the only factor affecting the variation among the states.

The wealth of the state conditions the extent to which it can be generous to those in need, however serious the need may be. Note, however, that the variations in wealth between the states, at least as measured by per-capita income, are not nearly as great as the differences in the levels of aid offered.[9]

While he never attempts to assess the independent contribution of environmental and political factors, Lockard is aware of their relationship. In fact, he outlines a sequence of development.

The diversity or lack of diversity of economic interests in a state tends to be reflected in the prevailing party system and the mode of its operation. In the first place, of course, it is the diversity in part that creates the atmosphere for two-party competition, and the absence of diversity facilitates one-partyism. In the two-party states the anxiety over the next election pushes political leaders into serving the interests of the have-less element of society, thereby putting the party into the countervailing power operation. Conversely, in the one-party states it is easier for a few powerful interests to manage the government of the state without party interference since the parties are not representative of the particular elements that might pose opposition to the dominant interest groups. The parties do not represent the have-less element for the simple reason that politically there is no necessity to do so.[10]

Fenton does attempt to sort out the relative importance of environmental and political variables.[11] The policy outputs he examines are per capita welfare expenditures, per recipient Aid to Dependent Children, per pupil expenditures for education, and total per capita general expenditures by state and local governments. He finds that for every category of expenditures, strong two-party states spend the most money, followed by weak two-party states, and one-party states. These findings suggest that party competition affects spending. However, Fenton notes that the competitive states are also wealthier and more urbanized and that the states with the highest level of expenditures are more competitive, wealthier, and more urbanized. He attempts to untangle this relationship by examining the association between competition and spending while controlling for income and urbanism.

The relative importance of party competition varies according to the expenditure area. Aid to Dependent Children expenditures are very much affected by party competition. Party competition is much less influential in the areas of welfare and educational expenditures. Urbanism is more crucial in accounting for welfare expenditures, and income explains most of the variation in educational expenditures. Competition exerts virtually no influence over total expenditures by state and local governments. Income accounts for 80 percent of the variation in total expenditures.

In other words, the wealthier the state, the more it spent in toto. Thus, competition would appear to influence the direction (e.g., highways vs. welfare or education) rather than the amount of expenditures, with strongly competitive states tending to allocate a larger share of their fiscal pies to the categories that reallocate goods and opportunities. The evidence thus seems to support the notion that party competition focuses on, and causes greater concern about, certain kinds of welfare and education programs than is the case in other kinds of politics. It is not proven, but it is a logical and persuasive conclusion, that this tendency is a result of the fact that party competition "democratizes" politics by paying greater deference to the poor and thereby rendering politics less oligarchical.[12]

In a different work, Fenton contends that these patterns are stronger in two-party states with issue-oriented politics than in two-party states with job-oriented politics.[13]

Further support for the importance of party competition in the determination of welfare policies is presented by Lockard in a later work.[14] Controlling for income, he finds that party competition is related to expenditures for six welfare programs. Lockard also examines the association between four nonexpenditure policies of interest to the have-nots—minimum wage laws, antidiscrimination statutes, small-loan laws, and the absence of right-to-work laws—and party competition. He finds a relationship between competition and these policies, with the exception of small-loan laws. The incidence of adoption of minimum wage and antidiscrimination laws is higher in the more competitive states while the incidence of adoption of right-to-work laws is lower.

That party competition is an important determinant of state policy outputs, especially those benefiting the have-nots, has been attested to by others. Pulsipher and Weatherby report that increased competition is associated with higher total expenditures by state and local governments as well as higher expenditures for education and welfare.[15] Casstevens and Press find that party competition is associated with higher per capita welfare and average old age assistance payments.[16] Party competition has a positive correlation with an antidiscrimination scale developed by McCrone and Cnudde.[17] In their causal model, a small proportion of blacks is correlated with greater party competition, which, in turn, leads to the passage of antidiscrimination legislation.

In a study of redistributive policy, Booms and Halldorson discovered that party competition leads to greater redistribution.[18] Richard DeLeon documents a more complex relationship between party competition and redistribution.[19] Not only is party competition (and labor unionism) crucial, but so also is an economic surplus to redistribute. As DeLeon explains:

(1) mass political organizations have little redistributive impact lacking an economic surplus to redistribute; (2) economic surplus, where it exists, will not be redistributed in the absence of mass political organization; (3) economic surplus and mass political organization both appear to be necessary conditions for government redistribution—neither by itself appears sufficient for redistribution to occur; and (4) mass political organization and economic surplus together do seem to constitute a sufficient condition for high levels of government redistribution.[20]

Using path analysis, Gary Tompkins discovers a strong direct relationship between party competition and per recipient Aid to Dependent Children.[21] However, the strongest relationship in his model is between ethnicity and aid payments. Using a nonexpenditure measure of state urban policies, party competition is associated with higher outputs.[22] This relationship holds even when income is controlled for, and is still quite strong when urbanization is controlled for.

Increased party competition does seem to affect policy outputs. But perhaps the effects of increased competition are not uniform; perhaps increases in competition will produce varying changes in policy outputs among the states. Using a nonlinear model, Gerald Wright produces support for the hypothesis that increases in party competition will be associated with greater policy differences in competitive states than in noncompetitive states.[23] Small differences in party competition have relatively little impact on policy outputs in noncompetitive states, but relatively significant impact in competitive states. The impact of competition is greater when the minority party has a chance to win. In such a situation, a modest increase in the share of the vote by the minority party could produce victory. Conversely, a small increase in the proportion of the vote garnered by a hopeless minority party will not alter the competitive balance. Where both parties have an opportunity to win, increases in competition might produce significant changes in policy as both parties jockey for the crucial votes that could produce victory.

Others have challenged the findings linking party competition and policy outputs. One of the initial challenges was Dawson and Robinson's ground-breaking article.[24] They tested the proposition that greater party competition is associated with more liberal social welfare policies. Contrary to the expected relationship, they discovered that

> high levels of inter-party competition are highly related both to socio-economic factors and to social welfare legislation, but the degree of inter-party competition does not seem to possess the important intervening influence between socio-economic factors and liberal welfare programs that our original hypothesis predicted. In short, the evidence points to the relatively greater influence of certain external conditions over one aspect of the political process in the formulation of welfare policies.[25]

In a subsequent article, Dawson examines the developmental sequence among environment, party competition, and more liberal policy outputs.[26]

> More specifically, a competitive party system serves as one of the basic mechanisms through which a diversified society makes its demands and resolves its conflicts in the political arena. It is especially a means through which the less socially and economically advantaged population groupings are brought into political participation and given a chance to exert political influence.[27]

Dawson examines these relationships in three separate time periods.

Dawson finds that party competition is related to socioeconomic conditions, especially during the last two time periods. Party competition is related to policy, with the relationship increasing in strength from the first time period through the third period. The socioeconomic factors are strongly correlated with policy outputs in all three periods. The socioeconomic factors are more strongly and consistently related to policy than is party competition. Dawson's findings are summarized in Figure 4.1. They portray diagrammatically his conclusions that

> socio-economic factors have been related to policy outputs over time regardless of the level of inter-party competition. More highly developed states become more competitive politically, and party competition has

FIGURE 4.1. Relationships between Three Sets of Variables over Three Time Periods

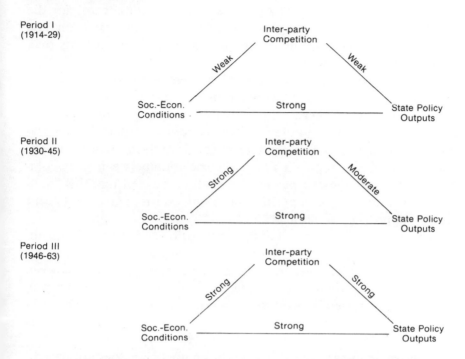

Source: Richard E. Dawson, "Social Development, Party Competition, and Policy," in *American Party Systems: Stages of Political Development*, ed. William Nisbet Chambers and Walter Dean Burnham (New York: Oxford University Press, 1975), p. 236.

become more closely associated with policy outputs in a similar way. The developmental findings do not allow us to affirm that inter-party competition has played any role in the development of more liberal policies. What they do suggest is that wealthy, urbanized, and ethnically diversified states tend to be more liberal in their public policies, regardless of the level of party competition. . . . High levels of party competition and liberal state policies both seem to be related independently to highly developed socio-economic conditions.[28]

After examining more extensive data than either Dawson and Robinson or Dawson, Dye arrives at the same conclusion.[29] Twenty-six of his fifty-four policy measures are significantly related to party competition when simple correlations are examined. However, only two of the fifty-four measures are significantly related to party competition when partial correlations are employed to control for the influence of economic development. Dye contends that economic development is more influential in determining policy outputs than is party competition.

In an article of major importance in stressing the preeminence of political variables in the determination of redistributive policy, Fry and Winters obtain a negative correlation between party competition and their redistributive index.[30] This is contrary to their expectations. In a methodologically sophisticated study of redistribution, Uslaner and Weber report a negative correlation between party competition and an index of need.[31] The authors suggest that this "indicates that interparty competition does not lead to a greater concern for the support of the poor."[32]

The effects of changes in party competition and changes in spending in several important areas of state expenditures have been examined.[33] Only low, and generally negative, relationships exist between increases in party competition and changes in the amount and proportion spent on public welfare. This implies that greater party competition does not necessarily lead to policies that benefit the have-nots.

Edward Jennings argues that party competition does not have to lead to more liberal welfare policies.[34] More liberal policies will result only if a lower-class party gains control of the government. In fact, if a lower-class party is the dominant party, a lack of competition could lead to more liberal policies. Using the terminology we have employed, if a party backed by the have-nots of a society gains power more liberal welfare policies should result.

Jennings examines six states with class-based parties and two states without class-based parties. His policy measure is per recipient expenditure of state funds for welfare. As he expected, the six states with class-based parties have welfare expenditures that are significantly higher than the expenditures in the two states without class-based parties. In over 80 percent of the cases, welfare policy is more generous when control of state government is divided or when a working-class party has control than when a middle-class party has control. Jennings finds that change in partisan control is related to policy outputs even when changes in economic resources are controlled for. However, Jennings's data leave much of the variation unexplained. As an illustration, 39 percent of the time when a middle- and upper-class party controls government welfare benefits increase.

A longitudinal study of the relationship between policy outputs and partisan characteristics of political systems fails to discern any relationship between party competition and expenditures.[35] Four political characteristics and seven expenditure characteristics are employed in the study, which covers the years 1946 to 1974. No consistent association is discovered among the independent and dependent variables.

> The inconsistency should put to rest the general notion that competition and expenditures are directly related. For states like Massachusetts, increased expenditures are associated with a decrease in competition, which no one has ever suggested should be the case. In a state such as Wyoming, the expenditures go up regardless of the fact that competition is increasing in the upper house and decreasing in both the lower house and governorship.[36]

The evidence linking party competition with policy outputs is mixed. The lack of congruence among the empirical studies can be attributed in part to researchers using different measures for the independent and dependent variables and employing different methodologies.[37] It is also not unreasonable to assume that the influence of party competition varies according to policy area and time period. One policy area where party competition has been expected to be particularly important is the welfare policy area. But even here conflicting empirical data have been offered. Perhaps the influence of party competition varies even among specific policies within general policy areas, such as welfare.

Those who accept the contentions of Key, Lockard, and Fenton that competitive parties are vital elements in the policymaking process must be less than reassured by some of the subsequent empirical analyses. Likewise, the theoretical attractiveness and findings of the works of Key, Lockard, and Fenton make difficult the unequivocal acceptance of the proposition, offered by Dawson and Robinson and Dye, among others, that party competition is relatively unimportant. The student of the state policymaking process is confronted with strong theoretical and anecdotal reasons for assuming the importance of party competition. Some empirical data buttress the theoretical propositions. But the student is also faced with strong empirical evidence arguing against the significance of competition between the parties. The jury is still out on the impact of party competition on policy outputs.

PARTISAN CONTROL OF GOVERNMENT

Many Americans treat elections as if they mattered. While voter turnout is not impressive in many elections, a significant number of those who do trek to the polls on election day are highly motivated. They believe that it really does matter who wins. Such partisans see the state prospering under the farsighted programs and sagacious leadership of their candidate and his or her party and withering under the ill-advised policies and inept tutelage of their candidate's opponent and his or her party. Others, who never get to the polls for one reason or another, are still willing to discuss the merits of the opposing candidates and to offer predictions about what will happen if one party or the other wins.

More sophisticated observers of the political scene react in much the same way. Political writers assess the implications of victory or defeat by particular candidates and parties. Political scientists discuss the far-reaching implications of particular elections. But does it really matter in terms of policy which party controls state government? A number of empirical studies have examined this question.

The pledges made in party platforms suggest that parties really do stand for different things.[38] One-party pledges are the most frequent type that occur in the platforms of parties in Wisconsin and Illinois. A one-party pledge occurs when one party takes a position on some issue and there is no counterpart in the platform of the other party. Such pledges indicate that the two parties have different sets of priorities. At the other extreme are bipartisan pledges, where the parties take essentially the same stand on a particular issue. Bipartisan pledges are fulfilled more often than are one-party pledges.

The policy consequences of differential partisan control are most obvious in the fulfillment of one-party pledges. Even controlling just one house of the legislature significantly increases the rate of fulfillment. Thus, "Differential partisan control of state policymaking institutions does make a difference in the sorts of policies which emerge from such institutions."[39]

The fulfillment of pledges was positively correlated with party control in Wisconsin. When one party controlled both houses of the legislature it was notably more successful in fulfilling pledges that differed from the pledges made by the opposing party. This relationship was weaker in Illinois, "indicating that other conditions, especially adequate party legislative cohesion, must be present for increases in legislative strength to have maximum policy impact."[40]

Any political party will have a difficult time enacting its platform if it does not control both the legislature and the governorship. If an opposition party controls one of the other institutions of government it is in a position to frustrate the partisan policy objectives of its counterpart. V. O. Key has pointed out some of the problems posed by divided control of government.

> Yet it is evident that quite generally divided control encourages a good deal of maneuver for short-term partisan advantage. At times this takes the form of irresponsible grandstand actions, as when one legislative house appropriates with great generosity secure in the knowledge that the governor and other legislative house will be compelled to redress the balance in the absence of revenues. The arrangement provides ready and easy means for legislative extortion from the governor and the executive departments. Perhaps, most important of all, the scheme delays or forecloses certain types of policy actions.[41]

Lockard emphasizes the policy implications of divided control of state government. He finds that divided control is related to deviations in state spending from what would be expected given a state's level of income and party competition.

> It is quite significant, then, that in a high proportion of the cases where states deviate significantly from the expected there is much divided party control where the states fail to meet expectations, or, conversely, little or no division where the states perform as expected, or excel.[42]

Legislators set priorities among issue areas. Important policy areas are those where a large number of legislators believe that action must be taken. The legislators expect something to be done in these areas. Working with this premise, Wayne Francis has developed an index of policy success.[43] Success is achieved when legislation is passed in those areas that the lawmakers deem to be crucial and a lack of success occurs when legislation is defeated in such areas. His index of policy success is a passage-defeat ratio on issues considered crucial by the legislators.

The index of success is affected by divided control of government (see Table 4.1). Policy success, as perceived by the legislators, is lowest when divided party control exists. Policy success is highest where one party controls both houses of the legislature and the governorship, but the minority party has some strength. Policy success is low in states where one party dominates.

TABLE 4.1. Policy Success under Three Conditions of Legislative Control

Condition	Index of Policy Success	Number of States
Divided party control: Either the senate, house, or both are controlled by a party other than that of the governor	.63	16
One-party dominant: One party controls both chambers and the office of the governor; minority party has no more than 17 percent of house seats and no more than 14 percent of senate seats	.67	11
One-party competitive: One party controls both chambers and office of governor; minority party has more than 17 percent of house seats or more than 14 percent of senate seats	.75	21

Source: Wayne L. Francis, *Legislative Issues in the Fifty States: A Comparative Analysis* (Chicago: Rand McNally, 1967), p. 55.

Policy success is lowest when control of government is divided and the number of seats held by each party in the legislature is close. According to Francis, "Divided party control seems to make less difference when the legislature is held firmly in the hands of one party. Perhaps the governor from a minority party tends to resign himself to a program of cooperation with the legislative majority."[44] When one party controls both branches, policy success tends to be higher when the dominant party enjoys only modest majorities in the legislature.

A shift in partisan control of the legislature is associated with changes in expenditure levels for specific policies. Jones documents that "shifts in party control from Republican to Democrat (as compared with changes from Democrat to Republican control) tend to lead to greater-than-average increases in education and welfare expenditures and smaller-than-average increases in total expenditures."[45]

Partisan control of government is correlated with the amount of revenue sharing money allocated by states to the areas of education-welfare, highway-recreation-public building, and tax relief.[46] The only variable significantly associated with education-welfare expenditures is the party in control of the governor's office. Democratic governors tend to allocate a larger portion of revenue-sharing funds to education-welfare than do Republican governors. The party in control of the state senate has the greatest relative influence in accounting for allocations for highway-recreation-public building expenditures. Democratic control results in higher expenditures. Party control of the statehouse has the greatest relative influence on tax relief expenditures. The Republican party is more likely to use revenue-sharing money for such a purpose.

Evidence has also been produced to support the commonly held belief that the Democratic party is more supportive of civil rights legislation.[47] Adoption of civil rights legislation in nonsouthern states is three times more likely when the Democratic party controls state government than when the Republicans are in control or when there is divided control. Uslaner and Weber find that Democratic control is associated with redistributive policies that benefit the lowest income classes.[48]

Proenvironment legislation apparently also has a better chance of passage in a Democratically controlled state legislature.[49] Proenvironment voting is significantly correlated with Democratic party membership. On every roll call examined but one, a larger proportion of Democratic legislators voted the proenvironment position than Republican legislators. These patterns persist when controls are employed for constituency opinion and educational, occupational, and residential differences between Democratic and Republican legislators. The lack of Republican support for environmental legislation appears to be related to that party's support of business interests. Business groups frequently oppose environmental legislation.

The strongest challenge to the importance of partisan control for policymaking is mounted by Dye.[50] He finds that thirty-one of fifty-four simple correlations between Democratic party control and policy outputs are statistically significant. However, when economic development is controlled for, most of these relationships drop below significant levels. Still, some relationships do persist. Republican party control is associated with greater spending for highways and greater financial reliance on local governments. Democratic party control results in greater participation by the national government in education, welfare, and revenue.

Overall, however, Dye contends that "Democratic or Republican control of a state government is not a good predictor of state policy outcomes."[51] Dye contends that this is because the parties do not offer consistent programs from state to state.

Richard Winters concludes that party control makes no difference for the redistribution ratio in a state.[52] Marquette and Hinckley find no relationship over time between Democratic strength and expenditures.[53]

Gary Klass offers a possible explanation for the research that assigns little importance to partisan control of government.[54] Perhaps the impact of partisanship varies with other factors. He reports that an increase in the number of seats held by Democrats in the lower house of the legislature does directly influence policy under certain conditions.

> Increases in Democratic strength, particularly under Republican majorities, have a strong negative impact on education expenditures when taxes are constrained and a positive impact on tax increases when the costs of education are held constant. Thus, the model suggests the conditions under which party preferences do play an important role; that is, when there are external constraints on tax increase (e.g., in the form of Proposition 13) or external support for education (e.g., federal aid).[55]

To answer the question posed at the beginning of this section: yes, it does seem to matter which party controls state government. Evidence has been produced that indicates that Democrats and Republicans do pursue different policies. Voters may indeed be making important policy decisions when they cast their ballots for state legislators and governors. Of course, the policy differences between the parties need not be dramatic and might not exist on every issue. Still, differential partisan control of state government does seem to be related to policy outputs.

VOTER TURNOUT

The American electorate is made up disproportionately of higher-status people. Lower-class citizens are less likely to vote. This increases the possibility that lower-class viewpoints will be ignored when policy is being made. Officeholders know they fear little electoral retribution at the hands of such groups. Increases in voter turnout, which could in most cases be assumed to result from the mobilization of the less wealthy and less educated, should make policymakers more sensitive to the needs of the lower classes. Higher levels of voter turnout, then, could reasonably be expected to be associated with policies more favorable to the have-nots.

Little empirical evidence exists to indicate the importance of voter turnout. Turnout in gubernatorial elections is positively related to the percentage of change in state governmental expenditures over time.[56] However, turnout is not significantly related to current state expenditures. Greater participation is also associated with a more generous welfare policy.[57]

As was the case with party competition and partisan control of government, Dye finds that voter turnout has little impact on policy outputs.[58] All but six of thirty significant simple correlations drop below the level of significance when controlled for economic development. Dye's data suggest that economic development has a greater impact on policy outputs than does turnout.

A study of redistributive policy employing turnout as an independent variable offers little support for the proposition that increased turnout will be associated with policies more favorable to the have-nots.[59] Contrary to the hypothesized relationship, electoral turnout is negatively associated with measures of redistribution for the lower classes and positively associated with measures of redistribution for the middle and upper classes. This leads the author to conclude, "Apparently, the common interpretation of the meaning of the turnout measure is in error. Either the increment in turnout is coming entirely from the middle and upper income groups, or the proportion of the increment from those groups overshadows the potential influence of participation by voters from the lower income classes."[60]

If participation is broadened to include both individual as well as organizational participation, its impact on policy is found to be greater.[61] Individual participation is measured by indicators of voter turnout and organizational participation is measured by indicators of interest group strength. Weak associations are found between the individual participation variables and several measures of policy outputs; much stronger correlations exist between the measures of organizational participation and the measures of policy. Both types of participation are also related to citizen dissatisfaction; once again, organizational participation is more influential. Participation tends to reduce the level of dissatisfaction. Baer and Jaros's work suggests that participation can have a significant impact on policy. But their findings clearly show that organizational participation is a more crucial factor than individual participation.

Empirical evidence is largely lacking that voter turnout significantly influences policy outputs. Democracy may be enhanced when legions of citizens participate in elections, but there are few indications that such participation materially affects the content of policy.

LEGISLATIVE APPORTIONMENT

Political scientists assumed that before *Baker v. Carr* in 1962 malapportionment biased the policymaking process against urban areas. Rural legislators, overrepresented at the state capital, were held to harbor anticity attitudes, which made it difficult for legislation favored by urban interests to be adopted. Reformers contended that reapportionment would increase the number of urban legislators at the expense of rural areas of the state and lead to the passage of more prourban legislation. Since urban residents typically expressed liberal attitudes reapportionment was expected to produce more liberal policies.

Political scientists have given considerable attention to the relationship between malapportionment and reapportionment and state policies. Many empirical studies reflect on the influence of apportionment on policy outputs.

Pulsipher and Weatherby were among the first to establish a relationship between malapportionment and policy.[62] They found that malapportionment depressed expenditures in a number of policy areas. Walker contends that apportionment is associated with innovation in state policymaking.[63] His data indicate "that those states which grant their urban areas full representation in the legislature seem to adopt new ideas more rapidly, on the average, than states which discriminate against their cities."[64] Walker believes that this is attributable to the urban legislators' greater receptiveness to new ideas.

Frederickson and Cho report a stronger relationship between their measures of reapportionment and state spending than between their measures of malapportionment and spending.[65] Confirming the expectations of the reformers, reapportionment is found to correlate with increased spending for urban areas—as measured by state aid to local governments. The longer a state's experience with reapportionment, the stronger this pattern tends to be. These relationships hold up even when political, governmental, and socioeconomic control measures are employed. The authors continue:

> Perhaps our most interesting finding is that malapportionment is associated with higher state aid and with distribution of that aid in favor of rural interests. It appears that rural-dominated legislatures favored state aid as a means of offsetting the need to raise funds locally. The reapportionment analyses indicate a trend toward lower levels of overall state aid and the distribution of that aid on a less discriminatory basis.[66]

Reapportionment apparently can alter the way a state distributes its funds—with urban areas receiving a more equitable share.

Cho and Frederickson have also examined the influence of apportionment on nonfiscal policy outputs.[67] Their dependent variable is the congruence between public opinion in a number of policy areas and adoption or nonadoption of those policies. They employ the same control variables as in their previous study. Curiously, with the exception of labor rights policies and firearms control policies, they report greater congruence in the period before reapportionment than in the period after reapportionment. They are not able to explain these unexpected results.

Apportionment change measures are significantly correlated with policy responsiveness indices twice as often as are measures of malapportionment. In six of the eight cases in which apportionment change was correlated with policy preferences, reapportionment was associated with greater responsiveness to public opinion. Cho and Frederickson contend that apportionment is a significant factor influencing legislative responsiveness in certain areas of policy, especially civil rights policies and firearms control policies.

Another study has also employed nonexpenditure policy outputs—the adoption of a policy in nine different policy areas—to examine the relationship between apportionment in a given year and apportionment change on policymaking.[68] Significant relationships were discovered in the areas of racial equality, labor legislation, women's liberation, highway safety, parochial school aid, violence reduction, and welfare regulations, even when other political and economic variables are controlled for. Reapportionment was associated with the adoption of more liberal, urban-oriented policies.

A slightly different methodology is employed by Hanson and Crew in a longitudinal study of apportionment.[69] They employ a before-and-after test in those states that reapportioned at least one house of the legislature before 1965 while using those states that did not elect a reapportioned legislature before 1965 as a control group. The policy measures are per capita spending in five areas and the total expenditures allocated by state governments to municipal corporations over 100,000 in population. The latter measure is specifically designed to measure the impact of reapportionment on urban areas.

Per capita spending change in the five policy areas occurs in 52 percent of the possible instances in the reapportioned states and in 37 percent of the possible instances in the nonreapportioned states. Thus, while changes take place in both categories of states, greater changes occur in the reapportioned states. Similar, but less dramatic, changes are documented for expenditures allocated to municipal corporations. Thirty-four percent of the cities in reapportioned states receive increased allocations compared with 23 percent of the cities in the nonreapportioned states. The authors conclude that reapportionment is related to policy changes, but its impact varies according to the policy area. Because changes also occur in the control group of states, Hanson and Crew contend that reapportionment is not a necessary condition of policy change, but possibly is a sufficient condition.

Two models of the possible impact of reapportionment on state expenditures are tested by Douglas Feig.[70] He labels the two models the quick boost model and the rate increase model. The quick boost model assumes that the urban Democrats, who benefited most from reapportionment, would give a quick boost to those expenditures which they favored. Subsequently, the annual rate of increase would return to the level that existed before reapportionment. In the rate increase model, expenditure levels in areas favored by the party advantaged by reapportionment would increase over a period of years rather than dramatically in any one year. He examines two expenditure areas of interest to urban residents and legislators: state aid to local education and public welfare.

Feig finds evidence of at least one of the effects in over one half of the states in the education area and in every state except one in the welfare area. This suggests that reapportionment did indeed have an effect in these two policy areas.

A study of the impact of reapportionment on policymaking in Georgia offers support for the conclusions of the comparative studies.[71] One consequence of reapportionment was the election of more urban legislators who were more liberal than rural legislators. Also, there was an increase in the number of roll calls on which urban and rural legislators opposed each other, with the urban legislators winning more frequently. Many of these roll calls came on bills favored by urban interests. The author is cautious about attributing these trends exclusively to the impact of reapportionment.

> Some of these changes began before reapportionment; and all seem partially the result of such other variables as urbanization and the growing saliency of urban needs. . . . But because reapportionment has brought in more urban representatives, who are more liberal, and who are voting together more often, and winning more often, we conclude that to some unknown degree reapportionment has been a factor in observed policy changes since reapportionment. The direction of these changes, moreover, is consistent with reformist generalizations.[72]

An impressive body of literature exists to counter the claim that apportionment significantly affects policymaking. Herbert Jacob finds only weak correlations between three indices of legislative malapportionment and three policy outputs.[73] This moves him to conclude, "Our data demonstrate that malapportionment in and of itself is not associated with some of the major ailments of state politics."[74] Shaffer and Weber find that malapportionment has little impact on policy responsiveness.[75] Thomas Dye reports only weak correlations between malapportionment and thirty selected measures of education, welfare, and taxation policies.[76] Once again, economic development turns out to be more important.

Richard Hofferbert discovered little association between apportionment and either the "liberalness" of state welfare policies or state aid to large cities.[77] Brady and Edmonds uncovered little impact of malapportionment on state spending policies, including responsiveness to urban needs.[78] They stated "that the whole Pandora's box of evil consequences which supposedly result from malapportionment—from right-to-work laws to not spending enough on school children—really has little to do with malapportionment."[79]

A study examining ninety-seven counties within the thirty-eight largest metropolitan areas in the United States reveals only a minimal impact of reapportionment on the distribution of state funds among the counties.[80] Reapportionment was not accompanied by a dramatic change in the distribution of state funds between urban and suburban areas.

Another attempt at ascertaining the impact of reapportionment on urban areas examines the response of a state legislature to proposals for metropolitan reform.[81] At the same time that the makeup of the Colorado General Assembly was being altered because of reapportionment, the legislators were considering several proposals providing for the restructuring of the Denver metropolitan area. The data support the hypothesis that reapportionment did not increase the chances of reform proposals being adopted. One reason is that reapportionment brought to the legislature new suburban legislators who were in conflict with central city lawmakers on a number of issues, especially metropolitan reform.

California is the laboratory in which is tested the proposition that malapportionment is incompatible with a liberal-welfare orientation.[82] Little difference in welfare orientation is discovered between the malapportioned state senate and the more equitably apportioned state assembly. The liberal-welfare orientation of senators is less a consequence of apportionment than of the socioeconomic characteristics of the districts they represent and certain role orientations. Moreover, over one half of the high liberal-welfare constituencies are nonmetropolitan in character. This results in the overrepresentation of high liberal-welfare constituencies in the senate. Thus, contrary to what might be expected, "California's industrial areas, her minorities, her poor, and her aged actually have been, in some instances, grossly overrepresented."[83]

Even if reapportionment does produce policy changes, those changes might not appear immediately. Alvin Sokolow details several of the factors that mitigate against dramatic change.[84] One is that a legislature is a pluralistic policy system. Such a system "is composed of separate policy arenas, each of which is defined by a network of participants who have a special stake in the outputs of the arena."[85] Because the policy arenas are largely autonomous, reapportionment would have little immediate effect on most of them. Other factors that inhibit change include the influence of the legislative leadership (especially in making committee assignments), legislative norms, and the socialization of new members. According to Sokolow, "The influx of a very large number of new legislators can upset these patterns of stability, but only if the new members can effectively replace the leadership or otherwise revise patterns of legislative control."[86]

Perhaps reapportionment fails to produce dramatic changes in policy outputs because the policy bias associated with malapportionment was slight. Such a case is presented by Robert Erikson.[87] According to Erikson, malapportionment was responsible for a persistent, but slight, bias against urban areas within the states. He contends that the policy impact of this bias was only "trivial." Erikson states that reapportionment has had a slight effect on policy. Because the bias existing under malapportionment was so slight, there was no reason to expect dramatic policy changes. In part, the minimal impact of reapportionment can be attributed to the fact that it has not resulted in the election of legislators who are notably different from those who served in the malapportioned legislative chambers.

The earliest empirical studies were quite consistent in their conclusion that equality of apportionment had little impact on policy outputs.[88] More recent attempts to examine the relationship have produced mixed results. By selectively choosing materials, it is possible to make a case for either the importance of, or the lack of importance of, apportionment in the policymaking process. Perhaps the only way to accurately assess the impact of apportionment on policymaking is through a series of intrastate studies. We would expect the most dramatic changes to accrue from reapportionment in those states where the most severe malapportionment existed.

LEGISLATIVE PROFESSIONALISM

The Citizens Conference on State Legislatures (CCSL) undertook its extensive study of state legislatures because it feared that those institutions had lost their ability to function as independent, effective policymaking bodies. Many political scientists assume that more representative, full-time legislatures composed of better-paid legislators, having stronger committees, and assisted by more staff and research personnel should produce more responsive, more innovative policies. But does legislative professionalism have an impact on policy outputs? Do states with more professional legislatures produce significantly different policies than legislatures that are less professional?

The report of the CCSL concludes that professionalism does influence policy outputs. Specifically, "Highly capable legislatures tend to be generally innovative in many different areas of public policy, generous in welfare and education spending and services, and 'interventionist' in the sense of having powers and responsibilities of broad scope."[89] However, two of their dimensions, independent and representative, account for little of the policy variation among the states. These dimensions apparently are more important in affecting how laws are made than in what laws are made. The other three dimensions and the overall index of legislative capability are related to a variety of policy outputs.

Using his own professionalism index, John Grumm documents that political structure can influence the outputs of a political system. Under certain conditions, political structures can reinforce or inhibit inputs from the environment.[90] If one refers back to the mainstream model, there could be situations where linkages A, B, and C are all of approximately the same weight in influencing outputs. There would then exist a "process in which the environmental factors produce pressures and demands for a particular output, and at the same time, help to create the structural conditions which facilitate the production of the designated output."[91] Legislative professionalism is one of three structural characteristics employed in a causal model along with four environmental factors obtained from forty-five environmental variables and five policy output factors derived from thirty-one quantitative measures of policy outputs.

Legislative professionalism independently influences the policy factor welfare liberalism. Furthermore, "impressionistic evidence, plus some weak statistical support, strongly suggested that urbanization affects legislative professionalism in a direction that enhances the ability of the system to respond to demands generated by an increasingly urbanized population."[92] The significant relationship between professionalism and welfare liberalism was not repeated for the other four output factors.

Grumm has also conducted a quasi-experiment to try to answer the question, "Do structural and procedural changes in the legislature have any effect on legislative performance?"[93] Grumm was concerned with both the effectiveness of the process by which policy was enacted (how well did it address the needs to which the policy was directed) and the efficiency of the process (relatively how much in the way of system resources was used up in the process by which the policy was enacted).

Ten experimental state legislatures were matched on a state-by-state basis with ten control legislatures. The experimental states were those that had undergone the most legislative reform between 1967 and 1972 while the control states were characterized by legislatures whose structures and processes had remained substantially unchanged during those years. An index of legislative reform was developed based on changes in

> frequency of legislative sessions, limitations on lengths of legislative sessions, restrictions on special sessions, bill carry-over provisions, total number of committees in each house, number of joint committees in each house, provisions for open committee hearings, requirements for committee reports, total compensation of legislators, and expenditures on legislative services.[94]

Three types of policy outputs were included: welfare, public education, and health.

Legislative reform improved performance only in the area of welfare policy. And effectiveness improved much more than did efficiency. The differences between the experimental and control groups in improvement in efficiency were not statistically significant. Apparently, legislative reform does not affect all policy areas equally; Grumm suggests that reform effects might be policy specific. It is even possible that improved performance in one policy area might be accompanied by diminished performance in another policy area.

> Obviously, there are trade-offs here. Increased resources cannot be allocated to all areas at the same time. So our question should now be posed in a different way; it is not, does legislative reform have an impact on performance in general, but, does it have an impact on specific areas and what are these areas?[95]

Grumm's work offers evidence that political system characteristics are intervening variables that mediate the influence of environmental characteristics on policy outputs. Environmental influences are strengthened or weakened by the structures and processes that are the political system. Such a notion is reinforced by the research of Phillip Roeder.[96] His findings imply that legislative reform (measured by the Grumm and CCSL indices) is directly related to two types of policies: welfare spending and police spending. His model indicates that executive and legislative characteristics of states mediate between environmental factors and policy outputs. In other words, "institutional characteristics independently affect public policy, with socioeconomic variables only indirectly affecting policy through these 'political institutions.'"[97]

Edward Carmines describes another mediating role played by legislative professionalism—that of mediator between party competition and welfare policies.[98] Carmines expects that the linkage between party competition and welfare policies will be stronger in those states that are organizationally stronger and more effective. In such states there is a greater chance that partisan conflict will be converted into policies. Carmines views the legislature as the most important political institution for converting partisan conflict into policy outputs; therefore, the more capable the legislature is, the stronger the association between party competition and welfare policy should be. Carmines uses Grumm's index as his measure of the organizational effectiveness of legislatures.

As expected, the correlations between party competition and welfare expenditures are stronger in the states with more professional legislatures, even after socioeconomic variables are controlled for (see Table 4.2). The mean partial correlation for the states with less professional legislatures is .01 compared to .38 for the states with more professional legislatures. The correlations are considerably stronger for the states with more professional legislatures for every welfare policy. The data indicate that the relationship between party competition and welfare policies is largely contingent upon the degree of legislative professionalism in a state.

Using legislative compensation as their measure of professionalism, Asher and Van Meter find a strong positive relationship between professionalism and certain welfare policies.[99] These positive associations hold even when the data are divided into southern and nonsouthern states. These patterns were uncovered by using a causal model incorporating a number of environmental and political system variables.

States with more professional legislatures appear to be more innovative in policymaking.[100] States scoring higher on Grumm's

TABLE 4.2. Fourth-Order Partial Correlation Coefficients (Pearson's) between Interparty Competition and Welfare Expenditures, by Level of Legislative Professionalism*

	Legislative Professionalism	
	High	Low
	Controlling for	
	Four SES Variables	Four SES Variables
1. Education expenditures	.65	.18
2. Total welfare expenditures	.27	-.13
3. Old-age assistance	.02	-.14
4. Aid to dependent children	.54	.10
5. Aid to disabled	.31	.11
6. Aid to blind	.24	-.25
7. Percentage to public assistance supplied by state and local governments	.63	.18
Mean correlation	.38	.01

*Alaska and Hawaii not included.

Source: Edward G. Carmines, "The Mediating Influence of State Legislatures on the Linkage Between Interparty Competition and Welfare Policies," *American Political Science Review* 68 (September 1974): 1120.

index "adopt innovations more quickly than more amateur bodies largely because they are simply more capable of quickly considering, examining, and deciding on the innovations of other states."[101] Professionalism is the variable most highly correlated with policy innovation. Interestingly, professionalism is also related to innovation divergence; that is, noninnovative behavior. States with more professional legislatures are more capable of acting in their own interests, different from other states. This might result in their being decidedly more innovative, or decidedly less innovative, than other states. In turn, this can be expected to result in greater opinion democracy.

Legislators' attitudes about legislative professionalism are related to liberalism in legislators' policy attitudes.[102] Using two scales of their own to measure professionalism, the researchers then related these scores to legislators' attitudes on thirteen issues. Generally, legislators who favored a more professional legislature also held more liberal policy attitudes. While there were some exceptions, parochial school aid was the only policy area where favorable attitudes on professionalism were associated with a conservative policy preference. These relationships survived controls for perceived district competition and the typicality of the district.

One of the chief skeptics of the importance of legislative professionalism is Leonard Ritt. Employing the CCSL indices and data for state and state and local governmental expenditures, he finds little difference in policy outputs between reformed and unreformed legislatures.[103] He also finds that his policy measures have varying correlations with the different dimensions of legislative reform. In some cases, a policy measure will be strongly associated with one dimension of reform and very weakly associated with other dimensions. He sees legislative reform as having virtually no influence on policymaking.

In a second article, Ritt tries to overcome a criticism of earlier works assessing the importance of legislative professionalism. It was charged that earlier research did not allow enough time for the legislative reforms to produce policy changes. So this time Ritt employs 1974 rather than 1970 spending data.[104] This methodological change does little to alter his previous conclusions. Once again, he finds that legislative reform has little impact on policy outputs. He notes, "What should be even more perplexing for reformers is the fact that legislative improvement in one area may have positive benefits in some policy domains and negative effects in others."[105] Affluence turns out to be an important determinant of overall state expenditures; wealthier states spend and tax more than poorer states. Another important determinant is previous expenditures.

Lance LeLoup challenges and reverses the findings of Carmines.[106] Unlike Carmines, he uses the CCSL index rather than Grumm's index. LeLoup also examines policies other than welfare: state interventionism, tax progressiveness, welfare liberalism, per capita expenditures. His hypothesis is that party competition will be more important in states with less capable, rather than more capable, legislatures. In states with weaker and less effective legislatures, access to the policymaking process might be limited to the internal party organization. Thus, party competition might be more necessary to translate public demands into policies. In every case but one, the data confirm his hypothesis. Party competition is not unimportant in states with more competent legislatures, but it is more important in states with less professional legislatures. If LeLoup's findings are correct, party competition is a necessary link in the translation of demands into policy outputs in states with less capable legislatures.

A study that reexamined the CCSL data resulted in findings that controverted those of the CCSL.[107] The CCSL's overall index and five individual rankings were employed along with the same five policy measures used in the original study. Added were two control measures. One was an indicator of economic development and the other was Sharkansky's reformulation of Elazar's political culture summary scores for each state. When the relationship between legislative reform and policy was examined, with economic development and political culture controlled for, little independent influence of reform on policy was observed. Approximately the same results were obtained when the relationship between reform and several other policy outputs was examined. These results suggest that legislative reform has little impact on policy.

Like malapportionment, legislative professionalism is a structural variable that Shaffer and Weber find to have little influence on policy responsiveness.[108] Two case studies have discovered little association between professionalism and public policy in California[109] and Illinois.[110]

Uslaner and Weber contend that professionalism has a variable impact on redistributive policy.[111] Professionalism is more strongly associated with redistributive policy in Republican states than it is in competitive or Democratic states.

> For Democratic states, the interpretation of professionalism as a potential method for controlling the communications flow in the legislature may be warranted. For the competitive states, on the other hand, professionalism may indicate not so much a patterned flow of partisan information, but rather simply an open and readily available source of information on legislation. The more highly professionalized a legislature is, the greater the opportunities for all legislators to study individual pieces of legislation. Redistributive bills, which ordinarily might be passed over because they seem too controversial, might have a greater prospect of passing after members' detailed consideration. . . . Whatever interaction there might be between partisanship and professionalism in this model rests on the assumption that the party has enough pro-redistributive sentiment to mobilize. The Republicans show less concern for social welfare policy than any other group. Hence, they should be harder to mobilize than Democrats or legislators in competitive states.[112]

The relative influence of professionalism on policy might be conditioned by the partisan distribution of power.

Legislative professionalism apparently has some effect on state policies. Welfare is one policy area where professionalism might be important. States with more professional legislatures also might be more innovative. Conflicting evidence precludes making a much stronger statement than this. But the positive findings do suggest that professionalism might be an important factor in the determination of public policies.

INTEREST GROUPS

The literature describing the importance of interest groups and the techniques employed by lobbyists is more extensive than the literature assessing the importance of interest groups in the policy-making process on a comparative basis.[113] That is notable because many people believe that interest groups give shape to much legislation. Not infrequently, interest groups are perceived to exert undue influence on legislators. Charges are leveled that certain powerful interests are able to dictate the details of bills and that these same groups "own" legislators. Much of what is known about the role of interest groups in the states is drawn from case studies.[114] Some comparative studies do exist, however. Of particular importance is the work of Wayne Francis.

Policy success in the American states varies inversely with pressure group conflict ("There were at least two major interest groups who were at odds with one another over this matter.").[115] Legislators have greater difficulty drafting legislation to resolve crucial issues when interest groups are in conflict (see Table 4.3). When interest groups display greater agreement among themselves, appropriate legislation is more likely to emerge.

When Francis employs all of his determinants of policy success in a causal model, the importance of interest groups is clear (see Figure 4.2). The pressure group content of issues, which refers to the origin of issues, affects both the partisan content of issues and pressure group conflict in the legislature. Pressure group conflict, as just described, is inversely related to policy success. In the ten southern states, the actions of interest groups are of even greater importance. This is due to the lack of partisan conflict in the one-party southern

TABLE 4.3. Policy Success and Pressure Group Conflict
in the Fifty States

	Pressure Group Conflict (Number of States)			
	Very High	High	Low	Very Low
High policy success (passage-defeat ratio)	2	5	8	10
Low policy success (passage-defeat ratio)	10	8	4	3

Source: Wayne L. Francis, *Legislative Issues in the Fifty States: A Comparative Analysis* (Chicago: Rand McNally, 1967), p. 58.

legislatures. The correlations between pressure group content of issues and pressure group conflict, and between pressure group conflict and policy success are much stronger than the similar correlations for the forty nonsouthern states.

The influence of interest groups varies by issue area.[116] In some policy areas, lobbyists are a vital part of the policymaking process while in others their influence is negligible. Francis has developed three indices to gauge the influence of interest groups by issue area. The first index measures pressure group interest in important issues, the second measures pressure group conflict over important issues, and the third measures reliance on pressure group consultation under the condition of legislators' uncertainty. Index scores were computed on the basis of responses by state legislators in all fifty states. Table 4.4 summarizes interest group influence by policy areas. The numbers in parentheses indicate the number of times specific types of groups were mentioned by legislators.

Interest groups exert the greatest influence in the areas of liquor, labor, business, agriculture, water resources, gambling, and social welfare. In each of these areas, index scores fall above the mean. This means that interest groups evidence interest in crucial issues in these areas, are frequently in conflict with each other, and are often consulted by legislators uncertain about specific bills in these areas. In the areas of civil rights and taxation, groups are interested and in conflict quite often, but are infrequently consulted by legislators. In the area of education, groups are interested and are consulted, but infrequently engage in conflict. In the remaining areas, interest groups assume a lesser role in the policymaking process.

FIGURE 4.2. Determinants of Policy Success for the Fifty States (Party Control Not Considered)

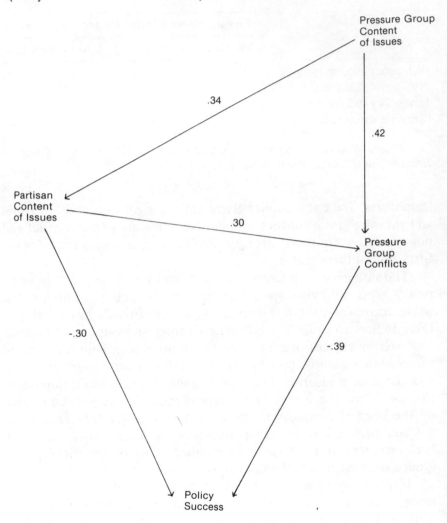

Source: Wayne L. Francis, *Legislative Issues in the Fifty States: A Comparative Analysis* (Chicago: Rand McNally, 1967), p. 102.

TABLE 4.4. Summary: Pressure Groups and the Twenty Policy Areas

Policy Areas	Issue Interest	Issue Conflict	Uncertainty Reliance	Powerful Groups
Liquor	.75	.65	.93	Liquor interests (124)
Labor	.78	.69	.73	Labor groups (495)
				Business groups (1,342)
Business	.69	.63	.71	Business groups (1,342)
Agriculture	.78	.50	.74	Farm groups (384)
Water resources	.65	.52	.83	Fishing industry (16)
				Paper companies (5)
				Utilities (183)
Gambling	.73	.56	.64	Gambling interests (31)
				Religious groups (39)
Social welfare	.62	.42	.62	Labor groups (495)
				Social workers (10)
Civil rights	.80	.59	.42*	Civil rights groups (19)
Taxation	.63	.48	.51*	Varied
Education	.72	.32*	.64	Education groups (510)
Highways—transportation	.50*	.32*	.62	Trucking companies (154)
Land	.60	.30*	.50*	
Finance	.47*	.27*	.24*	Tax and budget agencies (2)
Apportionment	.45*	.38*	.44*	Varied
Elections—primaries—conventions	.45*	.27*	.12*	
Local government	.42*	.33*	.29*	County and township off. (48)
Administration	.39*	.30*	.47*	Mun. associations (59)
Health	.39*	.17*	.50*	Medical association (37)
				Other health groups (13)
Courts—penal—crime	.35*	.27*	.46*	Bar association (23)
				Judges (12)
				Firefighters and police (13)
Constitutional revision	.47*	.33*		

*Value is below the mean for the index.

Source: Wayne L. Francis, "A Profile of Legislator Perceptions of Interest Group Behavior Relating to Legislative Issues in the States," *Western Political Quarterly* 24 (December 1971): 711.

Employing data from six states, three with strong lobbies and three with weak lobbies, Zeigler finds that the strong lobby states spend and tax more than the weak lobby states.[117]

Critics of interest groups have contended that interest groups distort the policymaking process. They charge that the policy goals of special interests often differ from those of the larger public. Thus, when legislators draft bills that incorporate the policy preferences of interest groups, policy is biased in favor of the organized, powerful few and against the interests of the many. Comparative data on the congruence between interest group attitudes and public attitudes is lacking, but one case study helps to shed light on this topic.

Interest group opinion was compared with public opinion in Iowa for fourteen state issues for the periods 1969–73 and 1977-78.[118] The two sets of opinions showed substantial congruence. Interest group opinion was basically reflective of public opinion. So much so that "on these issues and during this time period, legislators who responded entirely to the cues of concerned interest groups would not have substantially misrepresented the public in the policies enacted."[119]

The strength of interest groups does have an impact on state policymaking. Passage of legislation is more difficult in the presence of interest group conflict. Tax and spending policies are different in states with stronger interest group systems than in states with weaker systems. Group influence varies from issue area to issue area. And interest group opinions do not necessarily have to differ significantly from public opinion.

POLITICAL ROUTINES

Political routines are central to the policymaking process. Routines are "well-defined procedures that precede decisions."

> A routine is a rule used in making decisions that has the following traits: it is employed widely among people who make certain types of decisions; it focuses their attention on a limited number of the considerations that are potentially relevant to their decision, and thereby simplifies decisions that might have been complex; at the same time, it excludes certain considerations from the decisions, and contributes to political stability by making the decisions predictable under most conditions.[120]

The widespread use of routines makes a political system more conservative. Decisions tend to be made according to set procedures. Decision makers tend to rely on the same inputs during their deliberations and to exclude contrary messages from the environment. The predictability engendered by routines carries with it another benefit for policymakers. It enables some policymakers to correctly anticipate what others will do and to act accordingly. Routines are not easily modified or overturned, but occasionally decision makers do deviate from routines. Dramatic events are necessary to produce such a result. Included would be cataclysmic economic events, war, or dramatic events that result in political battles between the governor and legislature or in heightened public opinion. We will look at three political routines: incrementalism, legislators' reliance on the executive's budget cues, and regional consultation.

INCREMENTALISM

Incrementalism is at the heart of the budgetary process in the states. When reviewing agency budgetary requests, executives and legislators are most concerned not with the size of the request but rather with the increment of change. Those concerned with shaping the budget tend to work at the margins. What is of greatest concern is what is new or what is to be significantly increased from last year. Such proposed expenditures must be justified. What was in the budget last year and is being continued with only a modest increase in funding typically escapes intensive scrutiny. Last year's budget is perceived as legitimate. Last year's budget, or at least most of it, becomes the base for this year's budget. Attention, then, is focused on deviations from the base.

The routine of incrementalism has several advantages for policymakers. First, like all routines, it simplifies a complex task. This is particularly the case for legislators. State legislators frequently lack the time, expertise, assistance, and even desire to laboriously examine and debate the state's budget. Incrementalism offers a way to short-circuit that process. Incrementalism also enables policymakers to focus on figures rather than on programs. It is easier to vote for or against dollars and cents than people and benefits. A final advantage of incrementalism is that old battles do not have to be fought every year. Every program does not have to be rejustified every year. The base is accepted as legitimate and policymakers proceed from that base.

The result is that state budgets tend to grow gradually. Over time, total state budgets tend to remain in the same relationship to each other. This fact is dramatically evidenced by the data in Table 4.5. It shows the simple correlations between general expenditures per capita in 1965 and selected earlier years. The correlations are of a lesser magnitude the farther back one goes. However, differences among the states are statistically significant even for so long a period as 1903 to 1965. States that were big and small spenders in 1903 tended to be the same in 1965.[121]

TABLE 4.5. Coefficients of Simple Correlation between Current and Past State Government Total Expenditures per Capita

Years[a]	Simple Correlation[b]
1965–1962	.94
1965–1957	.85
1965–1952	.85
1965–1947	.63
1965–1942	.72
1965–1939	.61
1965–1929	.61
1965–1924	.53
1965–1918	.49
1965–1913	.52
1965–1903	.44

[a]The first year listed indicates the current expenditures; the second year listed indicates the past expenditures. The coefficients of simple correlation express the relationship between the two sets of expenditures.
[b]Significant at the .05 level.
Source: Adapted from Ira Sharkansky, *Spending in the American States* (Chicago: Rand McNally, 1968), p. 40.

The variable that correlates most strongly with current expenditures is previous expenditures. This is the case for total expenditures and expenditures for every major policy area except highways. Indicative of the importance of federal grants in this area, federal aid correlates most strongly with highway expenditures.[122] When a number of socioeconomic, governmental, and political variables are employed in a stepwise regression analysis, previous expenditures proves to be the strongest variable (see Table 4.6). The other two significant variables are the state percentage of state-local expenditures and local expenditures per capita. But, as can be seen in Table 4.7, the impact of previous expenditures varies from policy area to policy area.

TABLE 4.6. Coefficients of Multiple Determination Associated with the Most Powerful Independent Variables, as Determined by Stepwise Regression

Dependent Variable: Total State Government Expenditures per Capita, 1962	
Variables Added	R^2
Previous expenditures (1957)	.72
State percentage of state-local expenditures	.79
Local expenditures per capita	.95

Source: Ira Sharkansky, *Spending in the American States* (Chicago: Rand McNally, 1968), p. 68.

The variables employed by Sharkansky, which did such a good job of accounting for the variation in current state expenditures, do a poor job of accounting for changes in the level of expenditures. Periods of growth tend to be followed by periods of budgetary stability or decline.[123] This suggests that states are unable or unwilling to support dramatic increases in spending for a number of years. Changes in spending also are probably more dependent on idiosyncratic factors, such as the attitudes and resources of key politicians.

Asher and Van Meter find that incrementalism is important in explaining variations in welfare spending. Its influence is less in the southern states because of greater federal participation.[124]

The influence of incrementalism is apparently not limited simply to the budgetary process. Its effects can apply to the adoption of new policies. This is the conclusion drawn from an examination of the states' response to Economic Opportunity Act Programs.[125] In an attempt to explain interstate variation in response to these programs, variables were employed measuring established welfare policy

TABLE 4.7. Coefficients of Simple Correlation between Current and Past Expenditures, by Field of Service, 1957–62

	Current Expenditures for Field of Service
Past expenditures for:	
Education	.93*
Highways	.63*
Public welfare	.93*
Health and hospitals	.84*
Natural resources	.78*
Public safety	.70*
General government	.95*

*Significant at the .05 level.
Source: Ira Sharkansky, *Spending in the American States* (Chicago: Rand McNally, 1968), p. 42.

norms, economic development, and the electoral process. Established welfare policy norms account for the largest proportion of interstate variation, even when the effects of the other two classes of variables are controlled for. Perhaps

> economic and/or electoral characteristics of the states influence initial decisions of governments to participate in specific functional areas of public policy (in this case, welfare). However, once extensive involvement becomes accepted as legitimate, that established level of involvement is likely to independently influence response to new but similarly oriented policies in the states.[126]

Probably no political routine permeates the policymaking process to the extent of incrementalism. The importance of this political variable has been well established in the literature. An understanding of incrementalism is crucial to an understanding of the state policymaking process.[127]

LEGISLATORS' RELIANCE ON THE EXECUTIVE'S BUDGET CUES

For reasons similar to those that make incrementalism an attractive aid to legislators during the budgetary process, so too are legis-

lators encouraged to follow the lead of the governor when determining how much money to grant specific agencies. Typically, legislators lack the time and assistance to substantiate the myriad claims
put forth by agencies at budget time. How does one accurately assess
the merits of the various arguments offered to justify a larger share
of a state's funds? Most often, apparently, legislators prefer the view
of the governor to those of the agency personnel.

Sharkansky examines the budgetary process in nineteen states in
an attempt to sort out the relationships among state agencies, governors, and legislators.[128] His dependent variables are two aspects of
the budgetary success of agencies:

1. The percentage of the agency's request for the coming budget
   period appropriated by the legislature (short-term success);
2. the percentage of current expenditures appropriated by the
   legislature for the coming budget period (success in budget expansion).[129]

Sharkansky reports that agencies and governors are more consistent actors in the budgetary process than legislatures. Agencies
tend to request large increases in their budgets (15 to 31 percent)
while governors tend to reduce those requests (by 4 to 31 percent).
On the average, agencies request a 24 percent increase in their budgets, governors reduce those requests by 14 percent, and legislatures
appropriate an amount that is 13 percent less than what the agencies
request, but 13 percent more than what they are receiving under
their current budgets (see Table 4.8).[130] The final appropriation
tends to be closer to what the governor recommends than to what
the agency requests. This indicates that legislators look to the governor for help and that a favorable recommendation from the governor is vital for agency success. Also demonstrating the crucial role of
governors is the fact that a positive relationship exists between their
support and short-term budget success in sixteen of the nineteen
states and between their support and budget expansion in fourteen
of the nineteen states.[131]

Acquisitiveness on the part of the agency is crucial. Neither the
governor nor the legislature seems prone to grant large budget increases to agencies that do not request them. The rule seems to be if
you want money, ask for it. Agencies that request the largest increases
sustain the largest cuts, but end up with the largest increases when

TABLE 4.8. Annual Percentage Changes by States in the Budget Process of Major Agencies

State, Showing Years of Budget Analyzed and Number of Agencies	Agency Request as a Percentage of Current Expenditure	Governor's Recommendation as a Percentage of Agency's Request	Legislature's Appropriation as a Percentage of Governor's Request	Legislature's Appropriation as a Percentage of Agency's Current Expenditure	Legislature's Appropriation as a Percentage of Agency's Request
Florida 1965–67, $n = 39$	120	90	.93	109	84
Georgia 1965–67, $n = 26$	153	86	100	139	87
Idaho 1967–69, $n = 23$	119	93	92	109	86
Illinois 1963–65, $n = 37*$	118	83	102	108	85
Indiana 1965–67, $n = 47$	123	83	103	112	86
Kentucky 1966–68, $n = 28$	120	90	93	109	84
Louisiana 1966–67, $n = 32$	121	90	101	110	91
Maine 1965–67, $n = 17$	114	85	108	109	92
Nebraska 1965–67, $n = 10$	122	87	119	124	104
North Carolina 1965–67, $n = 61$	120	84	105	112	87
North Dakota 1965–67, $n = 21$	124	74	111	111	82
South Carolina 1966–67, $n = 29$	117	96	104	116	99
South Dakota 1967–68, $n = 25$	136	82	98	109	80
Texas 1965–67, $n = 41$	128	82	104	117	86
Vermont 1965–67, $n = 17$	121	87	106	115	91
Virginia 1966–68, $n = 57$	120	92	100	114	91
West Virginia 1966–67, $n = 43$	125	88	92	101	81
Wisconsin 1965–67, $n = 26$	115	96	98	111	94
Wyoming 1967–69, $n = 13$	133	69	109	112	75

*The Illinois data come from the Appendix of Thomas J. Anton's *The Politics of State Expenditures in Illinois* (Urbana: University of Illinois Press, 1966). All other data come from the official budgets and financial reports of the states.

Source: Ira Sharkansky, "Agency Requests, Gubernatorial Support and Budget Success in State Legislatures," in *State and Urban Politics: Readings in Comparative Public Policy,* ed. Richard I. Hofferbert and Ira Sharkansky (Boston: Little, Brown, 1971), p. 330.

the process is completed. Conversely, the governor and the legislature make only minor cuts in requests from agencies that seek only small increases.

How the governor and legislature deal with agencies, and with each other, is conditioned by certain political and economic factors. Short-term gubernatorial restraint of agency growth is associated with substantial veto powers and high state governmental expenditures. Legislative restraint in the short-term exists with relatively high state expenditures and a low incidence of separately elected state officials. Gubernatorial concurrence in budgetary expansion occurs with low state debt, high personal income, relatively intense party competition, and high voter turnout. Legislative acceptance of budgetary expansion tends to occur in concert with low total state expenditures and low state debt. There exists a higher incidence of gubernatorial-legislative rapport on short-term success when the governor has better tenure potential and there are fewer separately elected state officials and higher total expenditures. Agreement between the governor and the legislature on budgetary expansion is associated with high tenure potential and low state debt.[132]

Sharkansky posits three alternative causal models to sort out the relationships among the agencies, the governor, and the legislature (see Figure 4.3). The relative values of the alternative models are tested in Georgia and Wisconsin. Forty-three separate agencies in the two states, under different administrations, are the focus of the inquiry.[133] The model that holds most frequently is the first model—agency to governor to legislature. In Wisconsin, there are almost equal instances of the first model and model number three—agency to governor, agency to legislature, and governor to legislature. Model number two never holds. The models work better in Georgia than in Wisconsin, and better in instances of budgetary expansion than short-term budget success. The authors stress the importance of individual governors—the success of the models varies among administrations.

Deviations do occur from normal budgetary procedures. A governor may be motivated to support an agency's initial request, even to the extent of overlooking padding. The governor and the legislature may realize that a tax increase is necessary. This could lead to the acceptance of requests for increases. A governor may induce the legislature to support a program that he or she favors. The governor and the legislature may be willing to expand the budget of an agency whose responsibilities are increased by a new program, or they may react to curtail the growth of an agency that has a recent history of

FIGURE 4.3. Alternative Causal Models for Relationships among Administrative Agencies, the Governor, and the Legislature

Model 1: No direct link between agency acquisitiveness and Legislature

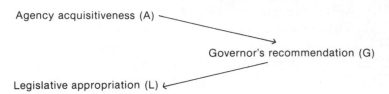

Model 2: No direct link between Governor's recommendations and Legislature

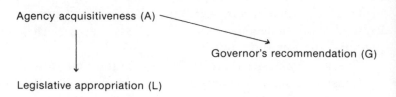

Model 3: Links from both agency acquisitiveness and Governor's recommendation to the Legislature

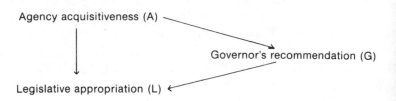

Source: Ira Sharkansky, "Agency Requests, Gubernatorial Support and Budget Success in State Legislatures," in *State and Urban Politics: Readings in Comparative Public Policy*, ed. Richard I. Hofferbert and Ira Sharkansky (Boston: Little, Brown, 1971), p. 334.

increases in its budget. Political disputes between the governor and the legislature may intrude on the budgetary process, making legislators less receptive to gubernatorial urgings. Finally, there exists a general bias against agencies with responsibility for taxation, law enforcement, and economic regulation.[134]

REGIONAL CONSULTATION

New ideas for policies do not have to originate within a political system. Some ideas are borrowed from other states; most commonly, from states within the same region. Policymakers look to their neighbors for policy cues for a variety of reasons.

> These include (1) the officials' belief that neighbors have problems similar to their own; (2) the attitude of officials and interested citizens that it is "legitimate" to adapt one's own programs to those of nearby governments; and (3) the structure of organizational affiliations which put officials into frequent contact with their counterparts in neighboring governments.[135]

It is reasonable and convenient to look to neighboring states for policy cues. Adjacent states tend to have similar social, economic, and political characteristics. There is every reason to assume that they share similar problems, and also that proposed solutions to those problems that worked in neighboring states can be successfully transplanted in similar political soil. Much consultation takes place among governmental officials within regions. Important forums are the meetings of professional associations whose membership is composed of state officials in various subject matter specialties. Formal presentations and informal discussions at such gatherings enable state officials to keep abreast of current trends. Policy innovations that have been tried and found successful can be extended to other states while those that have been tried and found wanting can be avoided.

Available evidence suggests that state officials do indeed consult with officials from neighboring states. Budget officers of sixty-seven major agencies in the states of Florida, Georgia, Kentucky, and Mississippi were asked whether they ever consulted with officials from other states about a situation they encountered in their work and which states they considered the best sources of information. The respondents identified 198 states that were considered the best sources of information. Thirty-five percent of the sources were states that bordered on those of the officials; 87 percent were states of the old Confederacy and Border states.[136] This implies that considerable consultation takes place among government officials within the same regions.

Officials of all states are not equally sought out as sources of information. Some states are perceived as more progressive and innovative, and their officials are consulted more frequently. Jack Walker has identified the states within various regions that tend to be the trend-setters.[137] The regional pace-setters are New York and Massachusetts in the Northeast, Michigan and Wisconsin in the Middle West, California in the Far West, Colorado in the Rocky Mountain region, and Louisiana and Virginia in the South. According to Walker, innovations diffuse among the states through a process of emulation. The states identified as regional leaders tend to adopt innovations first, and then these innovations are copied by other states for whom the regional leaders are reference states. Walker finds that while regionalism continues to exist, clearly defined groupings of states are less identifiable in the 1930–1966 time period than they were in the 1870–1929 time period. This is because new, more national channels of communication have been developed. States are no longer isolated from developments occurring in regions far removed from their boundaries. Regional consultation has been supplemented by national consultation. National standards accompanying federal grants-in-aid have also provided more national uniformity.

Sharkansky's data evidence greater uniformity of both national and regional spending (see Table 4.9). He states that this greater uniformity can be attributed to the effects of communications and grants-in-aid. Improved channels of communication result in emulation of both regional and national standards and programs.[138]

FORMAL POWERS OF THE GOVERNOR

As chief executives of the states, governors are potentially crucial policy leaders. Like the president, they can dominate the media. This enables them to make policy statements knowing the statements will receive extensive coverage. As leaders of their party, they are in a position to shape partisan policy. If they are in control of their party,

TABLE 4.9. Changes in Regional and National Uniformity: Coefficients of Variability 1902–62 for Total State plus Local Government Spending per Capita

Year	U.S.	New Eng.	Mid. Atl.	Southeast	Great Lakes	Plains	Mountains	Southwest	Far West
1962	.192	.119	.140	.141	.093	±1±	.189	.129	.095
1957	.219	.181	.146	.219	.091	.121	.148	.135	.137
1942	.292	.097	.207	.253	.077	.149	.070	.217	.082
1932	.378	.329	.275	.226	.152	.128	.204	.333	.268
1902	.672	.367	.371	.317	.152	.373	.247	.520	.573

Source: Ira Sharkansky, *The Routines of Politics* (New York: Van Nostrand Reinhold, 1970), p. 101.

or the dominant faction on it, they might be able to mete out rewards and sanctions, allowing them to dominate the legislative party. They may also have better information about policy options than do legislators. Such informal powers can make aggressive governors formidable figures in the policymaking process.

The various informal powers available to governors are augmented by the formal powers of the office. The four key formal powers are tenure, appointive power, budgetary power, and veto power. Governors with a longer term of office accompanied by the opportunity to be reelected have a greater chance to influence policy. Lawmakers and administrators who know that the governor will retain office for several years are forced to work with the chief executive. Governors who can appoint and remove key governmental officials will be more influential actors in the policymaking process. They will be able to appoint individuals who share their policy views and who will work to help them realize those policies. Beyond this, officials who owe their jobs, and the continuation of those jobs, to the governor will be more likely to support his or her programs. Governors who have control of the budget-making process have an advantage in policymaking. Finally, governors with a strong veto power will be formidable policy adversaries for the legislature.

Morehouse finds that stronger formal powers are positively related to more generous welfare policies and to greater change in welfare-education policy between 1968 and 1972.[139] Another important variable that works in conjunction with formal powers is the governor's party leadership. This is measured by the average primary vote the successful nominee of the governor's party obtained from 1956 to 1970. According to Morehouse, this indicates the ability of party leaders and gubernatorial candidates to put together a coalition that can control nominating and electing as well as the policymaking process. The coalition put together by the governor to secure the nomination and to win the election is the coalition that helps the governor to pass his or her policies. The larger this coalition, the more successful the governor should be in the policymaking process. The governor's party leadership is also significantly and positively correlated with higher welfare payments and greater change in welfare-education policy between 1968 and 1972.[140] At least in these two policy areas, a significant proportion of the variation among the states can be attributed to governors who are dominant within their parties and who have stronger formal powers.

Thomas Dye reaches a less sanguine conclusion about the importance of formal powers.[141] According to Dye, differences in expenditures for a number of state programs are attributable more to economic development than to the chief executive's formal powers.

SUMMARY

Empirical support has been mustered for the contention that political characteristics of the American states influence policy outputs. With the exception of voter turnout, a reasonable case could be made for the importance of each of the political variables examined. Some of the political variables are of significance even when employed in conjunction with environmental variables. That the studies cited are not uniform in their findings should not detract from the fact that at least for some policies, at some times, political factors are of consequence for the determination of policies.

The state policymaking process apparently is not devoid of partisanship. The level of party competition and the partisan balance in the legislature matters for some policies, at least. Whether state legislators are elected from urban or rural districts and whether those districts are equitably apportioned have also been found to have an impact on policymaking. Legislators serving in more professional legislatures have been found to arrive at different policy decisions than legislators serving in less professional legislatures. Legislators, regardless of party affiliation or type of district, rely on certain political routines in their roles as policymakers. Similarly, the party affiliation and formal powers of the governor seem to have an impact on the making of state policies.

The body of state policy literature that is frequently described as being unsupportive of the importance of political variables has been shown in this chapter in a different light. Empirical data exist that enhance the status of political system characteristics. However, the strongest support for the preeminence of environmental variables over political variables is found in a number of early studies that attempted to weigh directly the relative importance of the two sets of variables. It is to those studies and others testing the relative influence of environmental and political variables that we now turn our attention.

NOTES

1. E. E. Schattschneider, *The Semi-Sovereign People* (New York: Holt, Rinehart and Winston, 1960), p. 71.

2. V. O. Key, *Southern Politics in State and Nation* (New York: Vintage Books, 1949).

3. Duane Lockard, *New England State Politics* (Princeton: Princeton University Press, 1959).

4. John H. Fenton, *People and Parties in Politics* (Glenview, Ill.: Scott, Foresman, 1966); and *Midwest Politics* (New York: Holt, Rinehart and Winston, 1966).

5. For an argument that subsequent writers have attributed more to Key than he intended, see Eric M. Uslaner, "Comparative State Policy Formation, Inter-party Competition, and Malapportionment: A New Look at 'V. O. Key's Hypotheses,'" *Journal of Politics* 40 (May 1978): 409–32.

6. Key, *Southern Politics*, pp. 307–8.

7. Ibid., p. 299.

8. Lockard, *New England State Politics*, pp. 327–37.

9. Ibid., p. 331.

10. Ibid., p. 337.

11. Fenton, *People and Parties in Politics*, pp. 31–49.

12. Ibid., p. 45.

13. Fenton, *Midwest Politics*.

14. Duane Lockard, "State Party Systems and Policy Outputs," in *Political Research and Political Theory*, ed. Oliver Garceau (Cambridge, Mass.: Harvard University Press, 1968), pp. 190–220.

15. Allan G. Pulsipher and James L. Weatherby, Jr., "Malapportionment, Party Competition, and the Functional Distribution of Governmental Expenditures," *American Political Science Review* 62 (December 1968): 1207–19.

16. T. W. Casstevens and C. Press, "The Context of Democratic Competition in American State Politics," *American Journal of Sociology* 68 (March 1963): 536–43.

17. Donald J. McCrone and Charles F. Cnudde, "On Measuring Public Policy," in *State Politics: Readings on Political Behavior*, ed. Robert E. Crew, Jr. (Belmont, Cal.: Wadsworth, 1968), pp. 523–30.

18. Bernard H. Booms and James R. Halldorson, "The Politics of Redistribution: A Reformulation," *American Political Science Review* 64 (June 1970): 508–22.

19. Richard E. DeLeon, "Politics, Economic Surplus, and Redistribution in the American States: A Test of a Theory," *American Journal of Political Science* 17 (November 1973): 781–96.

20. Ibid., p. 795.

21. Gary L. Tompkins, "A Causal Model of State Welfare Expenditures," *Journal of Politics* 37 (May 1975): 392–416.

22. Michael LeMay, "Expenditure and Nonexpenditure Measures of State Urban Policy Output: A Research Note," *American Politics Quarterly* 1 (October 1973): 511–28.

23. Gerald C. Wright, Jr., "Interparty Competition and State Social Welfare Policy: When a Difference Makes a Difference," *Journal of Politics* 37 (August 1975): 796–803.

24. Richard E. Dawson and James A. Robinson, "Inter-Party Competition, Economic Variables, and Welfare Policies in the American States," *Journal of Politics* (May 1963): 265–89.

25. Ibid., p. 289.

26. Richard E. Dawson, "Social Development, Party Competition, and Policy," in *The American Party Systems: Stages of Political Development*, 2nd ed., ed. William Nisbet Chambers and Walter Dean Burnham (New York: Oxford University Press, 1975), pp. 203–37.

27. Ibid., p. 210.

28. Ibid., p. 237.

29. Thomas R. Dye, *Politics, Economics and the Public, Policy Outcomes in the American States* (Chicago: Rand McNally, 1966), esp. pp. 238–59; and "The Independent Effect of Party Competition on Policy Outcomes in the American System," in Crew, *State Politics*, pp. 249–60.

30. Brian R. Fry and Richard F. Winters, "The Politics of Redistribution," *American Political Science Review* 64 (June 1970): 508–22.

31. Eric M. Uslaner and Ronald E. Weber, "The 'Politics' of Redistribution: Toward a Model of the Policy-Making Process in the American States," *American Politics Quarterly* 3 (April 1975): 130–70.

32. Ibid., p. 158.

33. E. Terrence Jones, "Political Change and Spending Shifts in the American States," *American Politics Quarterly* 2 (April 1974): 159–178.

34. Edward T. Jennings, Jr., "Competition, Constituencies, and Welfare Policies in American States," *American Political Science Review* 73 (June 1979): 1414–29.

35. James F. Marquette and Katherine A. Hinckley, "Competition, Control and Spurious Covariation: A Longitudinal Analysis of State Spending," *American Journal of Political Science* 25 (May 1981): 362–75.

36. Ibid., p. 367.

37. See especially John H. Fenton and Donald W. Chamberlayne, "The Literature Dealing with the Relationships Between Political Processes, Socioeconomic Conditions and Public Policies in the American States: A Bibliographic Essay," *Polity* 1 (Spring 1969): 388–404.

38. Richard C. Elling, "State Party Platforms and State Legislative Performance: A Comparative Analysis," *American Journal of Political Science* 23 (May 1979): 383–405.

39. Ibid., p. 396.

40. Ibid., p. 401.

41. V. O. Key, Jr., *American State Politics: An Introduction* (New York: Knopf, 1956), p. 78.

42. Lockard, "State Party Systems and Policy Outputs," p. 206.

43. Wayne L. Francis, *Legislative Issues in the Fifty States: A Comparative Analysis* (Chicago: Rand McNally, 1967), p. 53.

44. Ibid., p. 55.

45. Jones, "Political Change," p. 170.

46. John J. Havick, "The Determinants of State Revenue Sharing Expenditures," *Journal of Politics* 37 (May 1975): 548–54.

47. Robert S. Erikson, "The Relationship Between Party Control and Civil Rights Legislation in the American States," *Western Political Quarterly* 24 (March 1971): 178–82.

48. Uslaner and Weber, "The 'Politics' of Redistribution," pp. 155–56.

49. Riley E. Dunlop and Richard P. Gale, "Party Membership and Environmental Politics: A Legislative Roll-Call Analysis," *Social Science Quarterly* 55 (December 1974): 670–90. Dunlop and Gale examine the Oregon legislature. Similar attitudes are reported among Montana legislators in a study measuring the opinion congruence between the public and legislators on environmental protection legislation. See Jerry W. Calvert, "The Social and Ideological Bases of Support for Environmental Legislation: An Examination of Public Attitudes and Legislative Action," *Western Political Quarterly* 32 (September 1979): 327–37.

50. Dye, *Politics, Economics, and the Public*, pp. 238–50.

51. Ibid., p. 247.

52. Richard Winters, "Party Control and Policy Change," *American Journal of Political Science* 20 (November 1976): 597–636.

53. Marquette and Hinckley, "Competition, Control and Spurious Covariation," p. 365.

54. Gary M. Klass, "The Determination of Policy and Politics in the American States," *Policy Studies Journal* (June 1979): 745–52.

55. Ibid., p. 751.

56. Ira Sharkansky, *Spending in the American States* (Chicago: Rand McNally, 1968), pp. 54–77.

57. Sarah McCally Morehouse, *State Politics, Parties and Policy* (New York: Holt, Rinehart and Winston, 1981), pp. 363–65.

58. Dye, *Politics, Economics, and the Public*, pp. 260–70.

59. Brian R. Fry, "An Examination of the Relationship between Selected Electoral Characteristics and State Redistributive Efforts," *American Journal of Political Science* 17 (May 1974): 421–31.

60. Ibid., p. 430.

61. Michael Baer and Dean Jaros, "Participation as Instrument and Expression: Some Evidence from the States," *American Journal of Political Science* 18 (May 1974): 365–83.

62. Pulsipher and Weatherby, "Malapportionment, Party Competition, and the Functional Distribution of Governmental Expenditures," pp. 1207–19.

63. Jack L. Walker, "The Diffusion of Innovations Among the American States," *American Political Science Review* 63 (September 1969): 880–99.

64. Ibid., p. 887.

65. H. George Frederickson and Yong Hyo Cho, "Legislative Apportionment and Fiscal Policy in the American States," *Western Political Quarterly* 17 (March 1974): 5–37.

66. Ibid., p. 35.

67. Yong Hyo Cho and H. George Frederickson, "Apportionment and Legislative Responsiveness to Policy Preferences in the American States," in

Democratic Representation and Apportionment: Quantitative Methods, Measures, and Criteria, ed. L. Papayanopoulous (New York: Annals of New York Academy of Sciences, 1973), pp. 249–68.

68. William R. Cantrall and Stuart S. Nagel, "The Effects of Reapportionment on the Passage of Nonexpenditure Legislation," in Papayanopoulous, *Democratic Representation and Apportionment,* pp. 269–79.

69. Roger A. Hanson and Robert E. Crew, Jr., "The Policy Impact of Reapportionment," *Law and Society* (Fall 1973): 69–93.

70. Douglas G. Feig, "Expenditures in the American States: The Impact of Court-Ordered Legislative Reapportionment," *American Politics Quarterly* 6 (July 1978): 309–24.

71. Brett W. Hawkins, "Consequences of Reapportionment in Georgia," in *State and Urban Politics: Readings in Comparative Public Policy,* ed. Richard I. Hofferbert and Ira Sharkansky (Boston: Little, Brown, 1971), pp. 273–98.

72. Ibid., p. 297.

73. Herbert Jacob, "The Consequences of Malapportionment: A Note of Caution," *Social Forces* 43 (December 1964): 256–61.

74. Ibid., p. 260.

75. William R. Shaffer and Ronald E. Weber, *Policy Responsiveness in the American States* (Beverly Hills: Sage Professional Papers in Administrative and Policy Studies, Vol. 2, Series No. 03–021, 1974).

76. Thomas R. Dye, "Malapportionment and Public Policy in the States," *Journal of Politics* 27 (August 1965): 586–601; and *Politics, Economics, and the Public,* pp. 270–81.

77. Richard I. Hofferbert, "The Relation Between Public Policy and Some Structural and Environmental Variables in the American States," *American Political Science Review* 60 (March 1966): 73–82.

78. David Brady and Douglas Edmonds, "One Man, One Vote—So What?" *Transaction* 4 (March 1967): 41–46.

79. Ibid., p. 46.

80. Robert E. Firestine, "The Impact of Reapportionment Upon Local Government Aid Receipts Within Large Metropolitan Areas," *Social Science Quarterly* 54 (September 1973): 395–402.

81. Susan W. Furniss, "The Response of the Colorado General Assembly to Proposals for Metropolitan Reform," *Western Political Quarterly* (December 1973): 747–65.

82. William De Rubertis, "How Apportionment with Selected Demographic Variables Relates to Policy Orientation," *Western Political Quarterly* 22 (March 1969): 904–20.

83. Ibid., p. 915.

84. Alvin D. Sokolow, "Legislative Pluralism, Committee Assignments, and Internal Norms: The Delayed Impact of Reapportionment in California," in Papayanopoulous, *Democratic Representation and Apportionment,* pp. 291–313.

85. Ibid., p. 300.

86. Ibid., p. 308.

87. Robert S. Erikson, "Reapportionment and Policy: A Further Look at Some Intervening Variables," in Papayanopoulous, *Democratic Representation and Apportionment*, pp. 280-90.

88. For a critical discussion of the "conceptual, theoretical, and methodological problems" plaguing several of the articles described, see William E. Bicker, "The Effects of Malapportionment in the States—A Mistrial," in *Reapportionment in the 1970s*, ed. Nelson W. Polsby (Berkeley: University of California Press, 1971), pp. 151-201.

89. The Citizens Conference on State Legislatures, *State Legislatures: An Evaluation of Their Effectiveness* (New York: Praeger, 1971), p. 77.

90. John G. Grumm, "The Effects of Legislative Structure on Legislative Performance," in Hofferbert and Sharkansky, *State and Urban Politics*, pp. 298-322.

91. Ibid., p. 301.

92. Ibid., p. 322.

93. John G. Grumm, "The Consequences of Structural Change for the Performance of State Legislatures: A Quasi-Experiment," in *Legislative Reform and Public Policy*, ed. Susan Welch and J. G. Peters (New York: Praeger, 1977), p. 201.

94. Ibid., pp. 206-7.

95. Ibid., p. 212.

96. Phillip W. Roeder, "State Legislative Reform: Determinants and Policy Consequences," *American Politics Quarterly* 7 (January 1979): 51-69.

97. Ibid., p. 63.

98. Edward G. Carmines, "The Mediating Influence of State Legislatures on the Linkage Between Interparty Competition and Welfare Policies," *American Political Science Review* 68 (September 1974): 1118-24.

99. Herbert B. Asher and Donald S. Van Meter, *Determinants of Public Welfare Policies: A Causal Approach* (Beverly Hills: Sage Professional Papers in American Politics, Vol. 1, Series No. 04-009, 1973).

100. Douglas D. Rose, "Citizen Preference and Public Policy in the American States: A Causal Analysis of Nondemocracy," in *Perspectives on Public Policy-Making*, ed. William B. Gwyn and George C. Edwards III (New Orleans: Tulane Studies in Political Science, 1975), pp. 53-94.

101. Ibid., pp. 61-63.

102. Eric M. Uslaner and Ronald E. Weber, *Patterns of Decision Making in State Legislatures* (New York: Praeger, 1977), Chap. 5, esp. pp. 144-46.

103. Leonard G. Ritt, "State Legislative Reform: Does It Matter? *American Politics Quarterly* 1 (October 1973): 499-510.

104. Leonard G. Ritt, "The Policy Impact of Legislative Reform: A 50 State Analysis," in Welch and Peters, *Legislative Reform and Public Policy*, pp. 189-200.

105. Ibid., p. 191.

106. Lance T. LeLoup, "Reassessing the Mediating Impact of Legislative Capability," *American Political Science Review* 72 (June 1978): 616-21.

107. Albert K. Karnig and Lee Sigelman, "State Legislative Reform and Public Policy: Another Look," *Western Political Quarterly* 28 (September 1975): 548–52.

108. Shaffer and Weber, *Policy Responsiveness.*

109. A. Wyner, "Legislative Reform and Politics in California: What Happened, Why, and So What?" in *State Legislative Innovation*, ed. James Robinson (New York: Praeger, 1973), pp. 46–100.

110. S. Gove, "Policy Implications of Legislative Reorganization in Illinois, in Robinson, *State Legislative Innovation*, pp. 101–35.

111. Uslaner and Weber, "The 'Politics' of Redistribution," p. 159.

112. Ibid., pp. 159–60.

113. For example, see L. Harmon Zeigler and Michael A. Baer, *Lobbying: Interaction and Influence in American State Legislatures* (Belmont, Cal.: Wadsworth, 1969); and L. Harmon Zeigler and Hendrik van Dalen, "Interest Groups in State Politics," in *Politics in the American States: A Comparative Analysis*, 3rd ed., ed. Herbert Jacob and Kenneth N. Vines (Boston: Little, Brown, 1976), pp. 93–136.

114. See, for example, William Buchanan, *Legislative Partisanship: The Deviant Case of California*, University of California Publications in Political Science, Vol. 13 (Berkeley: University of California Press, 1963); Andrew Hacker, "Pressure Politics in Pennsylvania: The Trucker vs. the Railroads," in *The Uses of Power*, ed. Alan F. Weston (New York: Harcourt Brace Jovanovich, 1962), pp. 324–76; Thomas Payne, "Under the Copper Dome: Politics in Montana," in *Western Politics*, ed. Frank H. Jonas (Salt Lake City: University of Utah Press, 1961), pp. 90–115; and Charles W. Wiggins, "Interest Group Involvement and Success Within a State Legislative System," in *Public Opinion and Public Policy: Models of Political Linkage*, 3rd ed., ed. Norman R. Luttbeg (Itasca, Ill.: Peacock, 1981), pp. 226–39.

115. Francis, *Legislative Issues in the Fifty States*, p. 58.

116. Wayne L. Francis, "A Profile of Legislator Perceptions of Interest Group Behavior Relating to Legislative Issues in the States," *Western Political Quarterly* 24 (December 1971): 702–12.

117. Harmon Zeigler, "The Effects of Lobbying: A Comparative Assessment," in Luttbeg, *Public Opinion and Public Policy*, pp. 224–25.

118. Norman R. Luttbeg and Charles W. Wiggins, "Public Opinion Versus Interest Group Opinion: The Case of Iowa," in Luttbeg, *Public Opinion and Public Policy*, pp. 197–202.

119. Ibid., p. 202.

120. Ira Sharkansky, *The Routines of Politics* (New York: Van Nostrand Reinhold, 1970), p. 3.

121. Sharkansky, *Spending in the American States*, Chap. 3.

122. Ira Sharkansky, "Economic and Political Correlates of State Government Expenditures: General Tendencies and Deviant Cases," *Midwest Journal of Political Science* 11 (May 1967): 178–84.

123. Sharkansky, *Spending in the American States*, pp. 73–77; and "Economic and Political Correlates," pp. 184–90.

124. Asher and Van Meter, *Determinants of Public Welfare Policies*, pp. 39–45.

125. Andrew T. Cowart, "Anti-Poverty Expenditures in the American States: A Comparative Analysis," in Hofferbert and Sharkansky, *State and Urban Politics*, pp. 413–29.

126. Ibid., p. 424.

127. But, in one important sense, incrementalism is an unsatisfactory variable. The establishment of a strong association between budgets does not answer the question of what the initial determinants of expenditures were.

128. Ira Sharkansky, "Agency Requests, Gubernatorial Support and Budget Success in State Legislatures," in Hofferbert and Sharkansky, *State and Urban Politics*, pp. 323–42.

129. Ibid., p. 326.

130. Ibid., p. 329.

131. Ibid.

132. Ibid., pp. 339–40.

133. Ira Sharkansky and Augustus B. Turnbull III, "Budget-Making in Georgia and Wisconsin: A Test of a Model," *Midwest Journal of Political Science* 13 (November 1969): 631–45.

134. Ibid., p. 235.

135. Sharkansky, *The Routines of Politics*, p. 86.

136. Ibid., p. 89.

137. Walker, "The Diffusion of Innovations Among the American States," pp. 880–99.

138. Sharkansky, *The Routines of Politics*, pp. 99–103.

139. Morehouse, pp. 363–65, 416–17.

140. Ibid.

141. Thomas R. Dye, "Executive Power and Public Policy in the States," *Western Political Quarterly* 27 (December 1969): 926–39.

5

POLITICS VERSUS
THE ENVIRONMENT
IN THE DETERMINATION
OF POLICY OUTPUTS

In the two preceding chapters, evidence has been presented that stresses the importance of environmental and political system variables, respectively, in the determination of policy outputs. It has been shown that both categories of variables do influence policy outputs. What has not yet been examined in detail is the relative contribution of environmental and political system variables in explaining the policy variation among the states. This issue has been a central one for the past two decades for political scientists concerned with the study of comparative state policymaking.

In this chapter, we will examine the empirical studies that have addressed this issue. Most of the earliest research stressed the crucial role played by the environment. These studies put those who argued for the significance of the political system on the defensive. Politics was portrayed not as unimportant but as subordinate to socioeconomic conditions in the policymaking process. Subsequent research has elevated the status of political variables. In some of the studies, the data even suggest the preeminence of political variables. At the very least, the relationships among environmental variables, political system variables, and policy outputs is more complex than the earlier studies implied.

THE CASE FOR THE PREEMINENCE
OF THE SOCIOECONOMIC ENVIRONMENT

Dawson and Robinson

As was mentioned in Chapter One, Dawson and Robinson's article was the first attempt to assess the relative importance of politics and economics.[1] Specifically, they tested for the relative importance of external conditions (wealth, urbanization, industrialization), political process variables (measures of party competition), and state social welfare policies. The policy variables were found to be strongly correlated with both the socioeconomic variables and the process variables. A strong relationship also was discovered between the process variables and the socioeconomic variables. After sorting out these relationships, Dawson and Robinson contended that the socioeconomic variables, especially income, were more important than party competition (see Tables 5.1 and 5.2). Thus, the initial foray into the politics-economics thicket discovered evidence for the greater importance of socioeconomic variables.

TABLE 5.1. Rank Order Correlations between Per Capita Income and Three Welfare Policies, Holding Interparty Competition Constant

	Per Capita Income			
Policies	Upper 1/3	Middle 1/3	Lower 1/3	46 States
Per pupil expenditures	.75	.70	.81	.88
Unemployment compensation	.37	.60	.41	.73
Old age assistance	.47	.46	.70	.69

Source: Richard E. Dawson and James A. Robinson, "Inter-Party Competition, Economic Variables, and Welfare Policies in the American States," *Journal of Politics* 25 (May 1963): 288.

Hofferbert

Instrumental in extending the argument developed by Dawson and Robinson is Richard Hofferbert.[2] His position is forthrightly stated in the second paragraph of his article: "The thesis advanced

TABLE 5.2. Rank Order Correlations between Interparty Competition (Average Popular Support Measure) and Three Welfare Policies, Holding Wealth (Per Capita Income) Constant

Policies	Average Popular Support for Governor, Senate, and House			
	Upper 1/3	Middle 1/3	Lower 1/3	46 States
Per pupil expenditures	.13	.34	.37	.64
Unemployment insurance	−.13	−.22	.41	.63
Old age assistance	.07	.24	.21	.53

Source: Richard E. Dawson and James A. Robinson, "Inter-Party Competition, Economic Variables, and Welfare Policies in the American States," *Journal of Politics* 25 (May 1963): 288.

here is that differences in policy, at least in certain substantive areas, are more readily explained in terms of differences in the socio-economic environments of the states than by an examination of structural variables."[3] Hofferbert examines the relationships among apportionment, party competition, divided control of government, and industrialization and the welfare orientation (the "liberalness" of welfare policies) of the American states. He finds no significant relationships between apportionment, party competition, or divided control and welfare orientation. On the other hand, he reports a strong association between industrialization and welfare orientation. Hofferbert concludes that "structural characteristics and, if one prefers to give partisan variables a separate berth, the nature of the party system and its operation do not seem to go very far toward explaining the kind of policies produced in the states."[4] He continues, "We see by the data presented here and elsewhere, however, clear indication that there is a relationship between environment and policy."[5]

Dye

Probably no individual is more associated with the point of view that environmental variables are preeminent in the policymaking process than Thomas Dye. In fact, one recent writer refers to the Thomas

Dye School.[6] Dye's position is developed most fully in his classic book *Politics, Economics, and the Public.* In it, he develops the basic policy model employed in the bulk of comparative state policy-making research. He presents extensive data to buttress his contention that economic development is more important than are political system characteristics in the determination of policy.

Dye's data reveal that economic development influences both political system characteristics and policy outputs. In addition, political system characteristics influence policy outputs. But what do the data reveal about the relationship among the three categories of variables? As Dye explains:

> partial correlation analysis reveals that these system characteristics have relatively little independent effect on policy outcomes in the states. Economic development shapes both political systems and policy outcomes, and most of the association that occurs between system characteristics and policy outcomes can be attributed to the influence of economic development. Differences in the policy choices of states with different types of political systems turn out to be largely a product of differing socioeconomic levels rather than a direct product of political variables. Levels of urbanization, industrialization, income, and education appear to be more influential in shaping policy outcomes than political system characteristics.[7]

Dye's findings are reported in Table 5.3. When statistical controls are employed, in virtually every case economic development is more important than the political system. The independent contribution of the economic development variables is typically more significant than that of the political system variables. But Dye cautions against assuming that political variables are unimportant.

> We are not really justified in concluding from this study that political variables do not have any impact on public policy in the states. We can only say that partisanship, party competition, participation, and malapportionment do not appear to be as influential as economic development in determining most of the policy outcomes we have mentioned.[8]

Lewis-Beck

Michael Lewis-Beck uses a path analytic model to test the comparative ability of the "competition-participation" and "economic

TABLE 5.3. A Comparison of the Effects of Economic Development Variables and Political System Variables on Policy Outcomes in the American States

	Total Effect of Economic Development and Political System Variables	Total Effect of Economic Development Variables	Total Effect of Political System Variables	Effect of Economic Development Variables, Controlling for Political System Variables	Effect of Political System Variables, Controlling for Economic Development Variables
Education					
Per pupil expenditures	.86	.85	.58	.61	.04
Average teacher's salaries	.91	.90	.43	.78	.05
Teachers with B.A.	.85	.70	.64	.54	.47
Teachers with M.A.	.64	.60	.33	.34	.08
Male teachers	.73	.70	.56	.32	.10
Pupil-teacher ratios	.80	.70	.74	.24	.30
Dropout rate	.91	.82	.79	.54	.48
Mental failures	.88	.79	.81	.32	.39
Size of school districts	.69	.52	.67	.05	.28
State participation	.74	.49	.70	.13	.41
Welfare					
Per capita welfare expenditures	.52	.41	.41	.12	.12
Per capita health expenditures	.57	.42	.40	.18	.16
State participation in welfare	.52	.41	.40	.17	.16
State participation in health	.57	.42	.40	.18	.16
Federal participation in welfare	.85	.85	.54	.62	.04
Unemployment benefits	.85	.84	.57	.60	.07
OAA benefits	.82	.74	.69	.37	.27
ADC benefits	.87	.80	.75	.44	.35
Benefits for the blind	.82	.78	.63	.43	.13
General assistance benefits	.86	.81	.66	.54	.24
OAA recipients	.62	.59	.41	.25	.05
ADC recipients	.66	.55	.50	.25	.20
Unemployment recipients	.78	.76	.43	.52	.09
General assistance cases	.55	.43	.44	.14	.14
Highways					
Per capita highway expenditures	.81	.75	.64	.40	.10
State participation	.56	.48	.34	.22	.10
Federal participation	.65	.65	.39	.35	.00
Funds from highway users	.50	.42	.18	.23	.09
Highway fund diversion	.59	.41	.31	.29	.12
Rural-urban distribution	.55	.52	.41	.16	.04
Public Regulation					
Government per population	.87	.83	.53	.66	.27
Number of bills introduced	.53	.48	.23	.25	.06
Number of laws enacted	.53	.48	.23	.25	.06
Public employees	.75	.73	.46	.46	.07
State employees	.65	.54	.25	.39	.19
Public employees' salaries	.88	.86	.44	.72	.12
Correctional expenditures	.78	.72	.34	.56	.19
Police	.80	.79	.26	.62	.38
Prisoners	.67	.27	.60	.14	.41
Crime rate	.77	.63	.28	.57	.33
Gambling revenue	.45	.40	.22	.17	.04
Divorce rate	.64	.37	.26	.24	.17
Parolees	.45	.49	.42	.28	.22
Taxation					
Total revenue per capita	.84	.81	.51	.61	.12
Total taxes per capita	.89	.87	.61	.66	.16
Debt	.71	.67	.40	.40	.07
State percentage of total revenue	.68	.40	.60	.17	.36
Federal percentage of total revenue	.71	.64	.39	.42	.17
Income taxes	.42	.32	.16	.15	.09
Sales taxes	.45	.33	.25	.15	.10
Alcohol and tobacco taxes	.40	.35	.25	.11	.05
Motor fuel taxes	.53	.38	.28	.23	.17
Property taxes	.80	.58	.73	.23	.46

Source: Thomas R. Dye, *Politics, Economics, and the Public: Policy Outcomes in the American States* (Chicago: Rand McNally, 1966), pp. 286–87.

resource" models to account for welfare-education policies.[9] He employs a three-variable model. His variables are economic affluence and Hofferbert and Sharkansky's competition-turnout and welfare-education factors. Economic affluence directly influences both competition-turnout and welfare-education policies. Also, it indirectly influences policies through its influence on competition-turnout. This leads Lewis-Beck to conclude that "when the effects coefficients for a common model of welfare policy are estimated in a data-based example, socioeconomic variables are found to be considerably more important than political variables."[10]

THE CASE FOR THE PREEMINENCE OF THE POLITICAL SYSTEM

Sharkansky

A landmark in the assault on the preeminence of socioeconomic variables was the publication in 1968 of *Spending in the American States.* Sharkansky's book differed from previous writings in that he focused exclusively on state governmental expenditures, in contrast to the combined spending of state and local governments. Some of his findings were in direct contrast to those offered by Dawson and Robinson and by Dye.

Sharkansky examines the ability of three different approaches to account for state governmental expenditures. The first approach is that of the economists, such as Fabricant and Fisher, to explain the variation in state and local governmental expenditures. The second is the efforts of political scientists such as Dye and Hofferbert to account for the outputs of state political systems. The final approach is the decision-making approach used to explain the actions of budget makers. Important in this literature are the works of Lindblom[11] and Wildavsky.[12] The lines of argument of the first and second approaches conflict with the third. The first two approaches stress the importance of economic influences on expenditures. The third approach suggests a lesser role for the environment. This approach stresses the acceptance by budget makers of a budgetary base and the use of incrementalism. To test the relative merits of the three approaches, Sharkansky employs forty-six variables measuring socioeconomic, political, and governmental characteristics of the states and relates these to a variety of policy outputs.

Sharkansky reports a number of positive relationships between the governmental variables and current expenditures for policies. More importantly, in light of previous research, primarily negative relationships exist between the socioeconomic variables and policy outputs. This suggests that the factors that affect state spending differ from those that affect state and local spending combined. Partial correlations were tabulated for the independent variables with previous expenditures controlled for and for previous expenditures with the independent variables controlled for (see Table 5.4). A number of significant relationships remain between the independent variables and policy expenditures. As was the case with the simple correlations, the governmental variables are positively correlated with outputs while the socioeconomic variables are negatively correlated with expenditures. What is most impressive, however, is the continuing influence of previous expenditures. While several of the independent variables also influence current spending, clearly the most important variable is the previous level of expenditure.

The same independent variables were related to changes in levels of expenditures. Basically the same relationships emerge, but the magnitude of the associations is weaker. Again, the governmental measures are positively associated with the dependent variables, while negative correlations exist between the socioeconomic variables and policy outputs. Previous expenditures exert little influence over changes in expenditures. The political variables' impact on expenditure changes is greater than was the case with current expenditures. Sharkansky accounts for this variation this way:

> The reason may be that the level of current spending represents an accretion of many years' time when the influence of economic and governmental characteristics have prevailed. However, at the point of deciding upon the direction and size of change embodied in a new budget, the interest of the electorate and the strength of the majority party might be salient.[13]

While current spending is best accounted for by governmental variables, changes in spending are influenced by a combination of socioeconomic, political, and governmental variables.

Sharkansky concludes that a political routine, incrementalism, exerts a predominant influence over policymaking. He maintains that his findings "argue against the claims of certain writers that eco-

TABLE 5.4. Coefficients of Partial Correlation between Current Total State Expenditures per Capita and Previous Expenditures, and between Current Total State Expenditures per Capita and Each of the Remaining Independent Variables

	Previous Expenditures[a]	Independent Variables[b]
Socioeconomic Measures		
Personal income (2)[c]	.85[d]	-.19
Personal income per capita (3)	.86[d]	.24
Urbanization (4)	.88[d]	-.41[d]
Population (5)	.84[d]	-.21
Population growth (6)	.85[d]	-.26
Labor force in manufacturing (7)	.80[d]	-.20
Value added by manufacturing per capita (8)	.84[d]	-.29[d]
Adults with college education (9)	.84[d]	-.28[d]
Families with low income (10)	.85[d]	.21
Population density (11)	.85[d]	-.31
Area (12)	.85[d]	.03
Nonagricultural labor force (13)	.86[d]	-.26
Nonwhite population (14)	.85[d]	-.11
Population foreign-born or of foreign or mixed parentage (15)	.85[d]	-.15
Political Measures		
Voter turnout for U.S. Representative election (16)	.84[d]	.04
Voter turnout for gubernatorial election (17)	.84[d]	.11
Party competition in lower house (18)[e, f]	.85[d]	.09
Party competition in upper house (19)[e, f]	.86[d]	.24
Party competition in U.S. Representative election (20)[f]	.85[d]	-.03
Party competition in gubernatorial election (21)[f]	.85[d]	.12
Gubernatorial tenure (22)	.85[d]	-.10
Legislative compensation (23)	.85[d]	-.19
Bills introduced per session (24)	.85[d]	-.17
Bills passed per session (25)	.86[d]	-.37[d]
Length of legislative session (26)	.85[d]	.02
Financial support of legislature (27)	.86[d]	.22
S-P index of malapportionment (28)	.85[d]	.05
D-K index of malapportionment (29)	.85[d]	.23
D-E index of malapportionment (30)	.85[d]	.09
Lower-house tenure (31)[e]	.85[d]	-.02
Upper-house tenure (32)[e]	.85[d]	-.07

	Previous Expenditures[a]	Independent Variables[b]
Number of legislators (33)	.86[d]	-.29[d]
Governmental Measures		
Federal aid (34)	.84[d]	.34[d]
Tax effort (35)	.82[d]	.42[d]
Income tax per capita (36)	.85[d]	.18
Sales tax per capita (37)	.85[d]	.06
Excise tax per capita (38)	.83[d]	.07
Income tax as % of total taxes (39)	.85[d]	.29[d]
Sales tax as % of total taxes (40)	.85[d]	.33[d]
Excise tax as % of total taxes (41)	.84[d]	.37[d]
State % of state-local expenditures (42)	.84[d]	.48[d]
% of state-local revenues to state (43)	.84[d]	.41[d]
Revenues from nonlocal sources (44)	.83[d]	.43[d]
Local expenditures per capita (45)	.83[d]	.15
Salaries of state employees (46)	.84[d]	.05
Employees per population (47)	.76[d]	.42[d]

[a]Coefficients of partial correlation in this column indicate the relationships of previous expenditures to current expenditures, while the effects of the corresponding independent variables are controlled for.

[b]Coefficients of partial correlation in this column indicate the relationships of the corresponding independent variables to current expenditures, while the effects of previous expenditures are controlled for.

[c]Numbers in parentheses refer to the numbered variables identified in Sharkansky's Appendix, pp. 156–59.

[d]Significant at the .05 level.

[e]These measures of interparty competition in state legislatures are not directly relevant to the nonpartisan legislatures of Nebraska and Minnesota. To obtain meaningful data for these states, scores obtained from a comparable measurement of competition for the governor's office were inserted as their scores for competition in the legislature. To cope with Nebraska's unicameral legislature, its competition score was inserted into both upper- and lower-house measures.

[f]All the measures of party competition actually measure the strength of the dominant party in state politics. For a measure of competitiveness per se, the reader might consider using the inverse of this variable. See Sharkansky's Appendix, p. 157.

Source: Ira Sharkansky, *Spending in the American States* (Chicago: Rand McNally, 1968), pp. 65–66.

nomics, above all, exercises dominant influence over the outputs of state (and local) governments."[14] He explains further:

> Writers who emphasize the economic correlates of public programs do not deny the influence of previous levels of activity. Rather, they ignore the influence of past decisions while seeking the constellation of factors that show strong relationships with current operations. When they claim that economics, more than politics, affects government outputs, they look past an obvious happening in the governmental process: the practice of public officials to accept established expenditures, taxes, or services and make decisions only about proposed modifications.[15]

Morehouse

Sarah McCally Morehouse presents an important recent argument for the importance of the political system in the formulation of policy.[16] In particular, she stresses the importance of strong parties and strong governors. She contends that states with strong parties and strong governors do a better job of providing for the needs of the poor, the elderly, children, and students than states with weak parties and weak executives. She maintains that political characteristics of states are especially important in the determination of redistributive policies.

Four political variables—participation, the governor's party leadership, the governor's formal powers, and legislative professionalism—account for more of the variance in welfare policy than the economic variable she labels integration. Welfare payments to children, the old, the crippled, and the blind tend to be higher in states where the governor's leadership and formal powers are stronger and where the legislature is more professional. Likewise, payments are higher in states where participation is greater. Greater participation suggests increased participation by lower status groups. When such groups continually are active and make demands, it becomes increasingly difficult for policymakers to ignore their demands for assistance. Such policies are more likely to be enacted in states where a strong governor leads a cohesive party.

Integration is an important variable, but its impact is more indirect. The influence of this variable is stronger in its effect on the leadership ability and formal powers of the governor than it is on welfare policy itself. In more integrated states—those that are more urbanized with more media circulation, and whose populations contain more people who are professional, middle class, educated, and literate—the governor is a stronger party leader and has stronger formal powers and the legislature is more professional. Thus, states with such environmental characteristics, reflecting greater complexity, apparently respond by providing their elected officials with stronger powers. Socioeconomic conditions influence governmental structures, which, in turn, filter the demands arising from the environment. This is basically a restatement of the mainstream model. However, in opposition to much of the research guided by that model, Morehouse contends that the political variables are more crucial.

> Welfare policy appears to be determined by a combination of socioeconomic, participation, and leadership variables. These influences taken together indicate that states with a high degree of professionalism, education, and personal wealth—as well as urban centers that spawn prob lems—tend to contain the elements of redistributive politics. It is there that the participation of low-income groups and the strength of the leadership bring about the provision of generous welfare payments to those in need. Apparently, both leadership and internal cohesion are required to mold policies like welfare programs, which bring about a wider distribution of the benefits of state expenditures across income classes.[17]

Change in welfare-education policy between 1968 and 1972 is also more responsive to political variables than to economic variables. Greater change occurred in states that had more professional legislatures and where the governor was a stronger party leader and had stronger formal powers. These political variables were stronger than the economic variables of integration and the Gini index of income distribution. According to Morehouse, these results reveal "that it is the efforts of the men and women in the political process that can represent the needs and demands in education and welfare and convince the people that the expenditures are necessary."[18]

An unabashed advocate of political parties, Morehouse is convinced that strong parties and strong political leadership are vital contributors to the quality of life within the American states. She offers empirical evidence to support Key's proposition that strong parties will adopt policies that benefit the have-nots. As she forcefully concludes her study:

The critics of party government who claim that social and economic conditions create the party system as well as the outputs of the state political process may still remain unconvinced by the test borings. It is true that the degree of industrialization in a state influences the needs and demands of its citizens. If the state has reached an advanced post-industrial condition, the quality of education may be higher and the smaller numbers of poor may be better cared for. The analyses in this book have taken these factors into consideration by testing all variables in relationship to each other. It is true that the wealth, education, and communication systems that exist in a state give rise to demands for political leadership and the formal powers and services to make it effective. In all cases, however, the economic conditions of a state have had less effect on the redistributive services than the combination of the political party and the political structures within which the party operates.[19]

THE CASE FOR A CONTINGENCY APPROACH: COMPETING MODELS AND MULTIDIMENSIONALITY

The writers associated with this approach adopt a conditional view of the determinants of policies. Policy is viewed as being multi-dimensional. In some cases, the environment and the political system also are portrayed as being multidimensional. The issue is no longer whether politics or the environment is more crucial in determining all policies, but whether politics or the environment, or some aspect of each, is more crucial in determining individual policies. Particular policies are the consequences of a complex interplay of factors. To varying degrees, individual policies are shaped by socioeconomic and political variables. The relative importance of each is expected to vary with the policy area being examined. The relationships among the environment, the political system, and policy outputs become much more tangled. But this is probably a more realistic view of the relationships. Three articles published simultaneously in the fall of 1969 provided the foundation for this approach.

Cnudde and McCrone

Cnudde and McCrone differentiate between two models drawn from the state policy literature.[20] Both outline a relationship among the socioeconomic environment, the political system, and policy out-puts. The first is referred to as the Key-Lockard, or developmental, model. It posits a developmental relationship running from the environment through party competition to policy outputs. It holds that party competition exerts a direct influence on policy. The second model is called the Dawson-Robinson, or spurious, model. This model is the predominant model in state policy research. It suggests that whatever relationship exists between party competition and policy outputs is due to the effect of the environment; the environment influences both party competition and policies. To these two models, Cnudde and McCrone add their own, the hybrid model. This model suggests that there are an unlimited number of intervening political variables between the environment and policy outputs. They propose to test their model using only one political variable, party competition. Their view is that it may be possible to reject the developmental model without having to accept the spurious model. According to the hybrid model, the socioeconomic environment affects policy directly and indirectly. As specified by the spurious model, much of the relationship between party competition and policy is attributable to socioeconomic factors, but some of the association, as contended by the developmental model, is attributable to competition itself.

The relative merits of the three models are tested in one policy area—welfare policy. Four welfare policies are examined: per pupil expenditures, old age assistance, unemployment compensation, and aid to dependent children. The welfare policy area is central to the conflict between the haves and have-nots discussed by Key. As such, party competition should have a good chance to emerge as an important determinant of policy.

Cnudde and McCrone find that the most appropriate model varies with the policy being examined. The spurious model is most appropriate for per pupil expenditure and old age assistance policies. The hybrid model appears to be the best choice in accounting for aid to dependent children and unemployment compensation policies. They also find that the four socioeconomic variables employed as controls vary in their impact on the dependent variable. How much each one reduces the relationship between competition and the dependent variable varies with the policy area. Thus, they urge caution in the selection of control variables. What control variables are selected could determine what results are produced. The authors observe:

as might have been predicted by Key, we tend to have different models with different policies. The extent to which we can reject the spuriousness model seems to vary as a function of the centrality of the policy to the struggle between the haves and have-nots. Our inferences therefore are consistent with the theory that given the advantages possessed by the haves, the organization, continuity, and visibility of alternatives provided through inter-party competition is important for the capacity of have-nots to attain policies in their own interests.[21]

Crew

Robert Crew factor analyzes expenditures in eleven policy areas in an attempt to develop categories of policies.[22] His analysis produces three factors that account for 60 percent of the interstate variation in spending in the eleven policy areas.[23]

Factor I is labeled "Rurality." Expenditures that load positively on this factor, such as highways and natural resources, indicate expenditures associated with a more rural state. On the other hand, expenditures that load negatively are more associated with urbanism. Factor II is called "Collective Orientations." The three expenditures that load most heavily on this factor are for welfare, health, and libraries. Crew states that the dimension characterizing this factor is a collective-individualistic one. Expenditures for health and libraries, positively loaded with the factor, benefit the entire community, while spending for welfare, negatively loaded with the factor, is intended to benefit individuals. Factor III is referred to as "Maintenance of Public Order." It is characterized by a strong positive loading for police protection. Strong negative loadings exist for libraries and education. Crew contends that "the dispersion of knowledge through education and library expenditures may be seen as an attempt to achieve order within society by perpetuating the values of the culture, including those habits, patterns of action, norms and outlooks that are fundamental to social and political order."[24] Because this is a different approach to achieving order than police protection, Crew expects these expenditures to load oppositely from police protection; this is indeed the case.

Crew next correlates nine socioeconomic and political variables with each of the dimensions of state spending. The nine variables account for between 24 and 30 percent of the interstate variation in spending. The relative effect of the socioeconomic and political variables varies among the policy dimensions. The socioeconomic variables are important in accounting for spending on the Rurality factor. The political variables are more important in understanding spending on the other two dimensions. Rurality spending is apparently influenced more by a state's socioeconomic conditions while spending for Collective Orientation and Maintenance of Public Order is determined more by political factors.

How can one account for the differential impact of the socioeconomic and political variables on the different dimensions of spending? In the case of the Rurality factor. Crew observes:

> Evidently, the conflicts, cleavages, and controversies associated with the rurality dimension have become so much a part of the activity of state political systems that their resolution has become an accepted part of the decision-making process at the state level and is limited chiefly by a state's socioeconomic capabilities, within the context of competing demands on scarce resources.[25]

Much less public agreement exists about policies on the other two dimensions. "The problem of maintenance of public order and the emphasis on the community as opposed to the individual have historically divided men of different political faiths. Consequently, the character and composition of political institutions are important for the resolution of these conflicts."[26] The result, according to Crew, is two different dimensions of policy outputs: "those partially dependent for enactment upon the nature of the state political situation and those generally favored policies whose extensive application is limited chiefly by a state's socioeconomic condition."[27]

Sharkansky and Hofferbert

Also employing factor analysis, Sharkansky and Hofferbert identify two political, two public policy, and two socioeconomic factors.[28] Here is further proof of the multidimensional nature of policy; but, beyond this, proof also of the multidimensional nature of the political system and the socioeconomic environment.

The first political factor is termed "Professional-Local Reliance." The positively loaded variables on this factor include judicial and legislative compensation, expenditures on legislative services, and legislative activity. Loaded negatively are measures of reliance on state governmental expenditures and federal aid. These states have well-paid judges and legislators, more professional legislatures, and display more reliance on local revenue. The second political factor is called "Competition-Turnout." The strongest positively loaded variables are gubernatorial election turnout and an index of liberal suffrage laws. The strongest negatively loaded variables are measures of one-party dominance of the lower house of the state legislature and gubernatorial elections.

"Welfare-Education" is the first public policy factor. Variables loading strongly on this factor include measures indicating high welfare payments, a higher percentage of high school graduates, and greater success by state residents on national educational examinations. The second public policy factor is labeled "Highways-Natural Resources." Its principal components include measures of rural highway mileage, highway expenditures, fish and wildlife services, and expenditures for natural resources. States scoring higher on this factor have more miles of highways and spend more for fish and wildlife management and natural resources.

The socioeconomic factors are referred to as "Industrialization" and "Affluence." The two measures that load most strongly and positively with the first factor are value added by manufacture per capita and percentage employed in manufacturing. Loading strongly and positively with the second factor are median school years completed, estimated value of real property per capita, personal income per capita, and motor vehicle registration per 1,000 population. Just as the labels imply, states scoring higher on these factors are more industrialized and have citizens who are more affluent.

The interrelationships among the factors are displayed in Table 5.5. Clearly, whether politics or the environment is more important in the determination of policy depends on the dimension of policy being examined. Even more than this, the dimension of the environment or the political system that is more important varies according to the policy dimension. For example, the Welfare-Education dimension of policy is most strongly correlated with one dimension of the political system—Competition-Turnout—and one dimension of the socioeconomic environment—Affluence. States providing higher welfare payments and better educational services are characterized by stronger party competition, better voter turnout, and higher levels of

TABLE 5.5. Coefficients of Simple, Partial, and Multiple
Correlation and Multiple Determination between Socioeconomic,
Political, and Policy Factors

	Welfare-Education	Highways-Natural Resources	Welfare-Education	Highways-Natural Resources
	Simple Correlation		Partial Correlation*	
Professionalism-Local Reliance	.39	-.54	.26	-.24
Competition-Turnout	.68	.25	.47	-.02
Industrialization	.37	-.69	.17	-.55
Affluence	.69	.43	.43	.53
	Multiple Correlation		Multiple Determination	
Socioeconomic Factors	.77	.82	.59	.68
Political Factors	.78	.60	.61	.36
Socioeconomic and Political Factors	.83	.84	.69	.70

*Controlling for the other factors.

Source: Ira Sharkansky and Richard I. Hofferbert, "Dimensions of State Politics, Economics, and Public Policy," *American Political Science Review* 63 (September 1969): 877.

wealth and education. The Highways–Natural Resource policy dimension is influenced most strongly by the two socioeconomic factors. States with more miles of rural roads and better wildlife management programs tend to be states that are less industrialized, less urbanized, and have less population density coupled with greater personal wealth and higher levels of education.

Sharkansky and Hofferbert's findings show clearly that the environment, the political system, and public policies must be viewed as being multidimensional. On the crucial question that has monopolized the attention of state policy analysts for the past two decades, they write, "There is no single answer to the question: 'Is it politics or economics that has the greatest impact on public policy?' The answer (contrary to the thrust of much recent research) varies with the dimensions of each phenomena that are at issue."[29]

Hopkins and Weber

In part, this work is a replication of Sharkansky and Hofferbert's study.[30] Sixty-six policy variables are factor analyzed; included are the twenty-six variables used by Sharkansky and Hofferbert and forty nonexpenditure policy variables. Fourteen factors are yielded by the analysis; the five most important are the focus of the study. The first factor is identified as "Civil Rights/Education/Welfare." States scoring high on this factor have public accommodation and open housing laws, spend more on education and have better educated populations, and have more restrictive welfare policies. The second factor is labeled "Natural Resources/Highways." States scoring high on this factor spend more on natural resources and have more highway mileage. These first two factors are very similar to Sharkansky and Hofferbert's two policy factors. The third factor is called "Welfare Payments." Variables indicating higher welfare payments have strong positive loadings on this factor. The fourth factor is described as "Public Employee Unionization/Capital Punishment." Loading positively on this factor are measures for collective bargaining among several groups of public employees and the presence of the death penalty. The final factor examined is titled "Expenditures/Highways." It is basically composed of spending measures but also includes loadings for some measures of highway policies.

In an attempt to determine the congruence between their first two factors and the policy factors identified by Sharkansky and Hofferbert, Hopkins and Weber calculate Pearson product moment correlations between the two sets of factors. The correlation between Sharkansky and Hofferbert's Welfare-Education factor and their Civil Rights/Education/Welfare factor is .73; the correlation between the two highways and natural resource factors is an incredibly high .99. This leads Hopkins and Weber to conclude that these factors have identified two central dimensions of state policy.

To try to assess the relative importance of the environment and the political system in influencing each of the policy dimensions, Hopkins and Weber correlate Sharkansky and Hofferbert's socioeconomic and political factors with their five policy factors. The results can be seen in Table 5.6. The dimensions of the socioeconomic environment and the political system affecting the first two factors are almost identical to the results reported by Sharkansky and Hofferbert. In the case of the Civil Rights/Education/Welfare dimension, the

TABLE 5.6. Simple Correlation among Policy, Socioeconomic, and Political Factors

	Industriali-zation	Affluence	Professionalism/ Local Reliance	Competition/ Turnout
Affluence	.039			
Professionalism/ Local Reliance	.738	.140		
Competition/ Turnout	.114	.674	−.002	
Civil Rights/ Education/ Welfare	.263	.672	.148	.722
Natural Resources/ Highways	−.781	.285	−.547	.173
Welfare Expenditures	.193	.241	.332	.100
Public Employee Unionization/ Capital Punish-ment	−.174	−.110	−.349	−.102
Expenditures/ Highways	−.156	.039	−.233	−.111

Note: Alaska and Hawaii were excluded.

Source: Anne H. Hopkins and Ronald E. Weber, "Dimensions of Public Policies in the American States," *Polity* 8 (Spring 1976): 486.

Competition-Turnout dimension of the political system and the Affluence dimension of the environment are most crucial. The Industrialization dimension of the environment and the Professionalism/ Local Reliance dimension of the political system have the strongest influence on the Natural Resources/Highways policy dimension. The other three factors are only weakly correlated with the socioeconomic and political factors.

The first two factors also are considerably different from the latter three when it comes to the total amount of variation accounted for by the socioeconomic and political factors (see Table 5.7). The results for the first two factors are again very similar to those reported by Sharkansky and Hofferbert. Characteristics of the socioeconomic environment and the political system seem to exert little

TABLE 5.7. Coefficients of Multiple Determination between Socioeconomic, Political, and Policy Factors, as Determined by Stepwise Regression

	R^2
Dependent Variable: Civil Rights/Education/Welfare	
Variables Added:	
Competition/Turnout	.522
Affluence	.585
Industrialization	.623
Professionalism/Local Reliance	.628
Dependent Variable: Natural Resources/Highways	
Variables Added:	
Industrialization	.610
Affluence	.710
Competition/Turnout	.714
Professionalism/Local Reliance	.715
Dependent Variable: Welfare Expenditures	
Variables Added:	
Professionalism/Local Reliance	.110
Affluence	.149
Industrialization	.152
Competition/Turnout	.153
Dependent Variable: Public Employee Unionization/Capital Punishment	
Variables Added:	
Professionalism/Local Reliance	.122
Industrialization	.138
Competition/Turnout	.153
Affluence	.156
Dependent Variable: Expenditures/Highways	
Variables Added:	
Professionalism/Local Reliance	.054
Competition/Turnout	.067
Affluence	.108
Industrialization	.119

Source: Anne H. Hopkins and Ronald E. Weber, "Dimensions of Public Policies in the American States," *Polity* 8 (Spring 1976): 487.

influence on the latter three policy dimensions. The authors suggest that these new policy dimensions do not seem to be shaped by the traditional determinants of public policy. Whatever determines these policies apparently has not been tapped by the variables so far employed in the study of state policy formation.

Asher and Van Meter

These analysts are concerned with two types of welfare policy: Aid to Families with Dependent Children and Aid to the Blind.[31] They employ a number of socioeconomic and political variables as predictor variables. Their data reveal that political variables are more important than socioeconomic variables in the determination of total welfare effort, with the exception of Aid to the Blind in the South. When only state effort is examined—federal funds are excluded from the analysis—slightly different results are produced. Socioeconomic variables are more powerful for state Aid to Families with Dependent Children for all states and for nonsouthern states. Neither the socioeconomic nor the political variables do a good job of predicting state effort in the case of aid to the blind.

Here is further evidence of the differential impact of different categories of variables, depending on the policy dimension being examined.

The relative importance of socioeconomic and political variables as determinants of policy outputs differs greatly from one policy dimension to another. For total Aid to Families with Dependent Children effort, political variables have greater explanatory power than do the socioeconomic variables, a pattern that is reversed for state Aid to Families with Dependent Children effort. This indicates that the availability of resources and/or the existence of need within a state have a greater impact on Aid to Families with Dependent Children effort where the contributions of the federal government have been excluded from the analysis. Neither political nor socioeconomic variables have substantial explanatory power for total or state Aid to the Blind effort, which is surprising given the limited costs and noncontroversial character of the program.[32]

Cho and Frederickson

The varying impact of environmental and political system variables is made quite clear in this sophisticated study employing 92 measures of fiscal policies and 67 socioeconomic and political-governmental variables.[33] Findings are reported for 1962 and 1969.

The 1962 results indicate that socioeconomic variables are more important for half of the expenditures and political-governmental variables are more important for the other half. For people-oriented policies political variables are more crucial while for land-oriented policies (e.g., highways and natural resources) environmental variables are more significant. The competing sets of variables are of equal importance in determining total expenditures and educational expenditures. For spending change from 1957–62, political-governmental variables are of greater importance in 6 of the 11 areas examined with environmental variables more important in the remaining five. Political factors are slightly more important in determining how rapidly spending increases.

The data for 1969 reveal an even greater role for the political-governmental variables. These variables dominate on 10 of 14 spending measures, and are of nearly equal importance in the other four areas. For spending change from 1962–69, political-governmental variables dominate in 10 of 11 policy categories.

When changes between the two periods are examined, a particularly complex set of relationships emerges among the variables. Socioeconomic variables, especially urbanism, decline in importance while several political-governmental variables gain in significance, notably apportionment, political participation, and political conflict. Some variables, such as economic development and government modernism, maintain a consistent relationship among policy areas and between periods; some variables, such as political participation and apportionment are consistently related to different types of policies within the same time period but differentially related to these policies between periods; some variables, such as urbanism and political conflict, display an influence which varies from one policy area to another within time periods and between time periods.

display an influence which varies from one policy area to another within time periods and between time periods.

Overall, the authors conclude that socioeconomic variables are more crucial in determining total taxing and spending policies. However, socioeconomic and political-governmental variables vary in their impact on specific policy areas. Socioeconomic variables are more influential for land-oriented policies while the political-governmental variables are more influential when the policy area is shared by state and local governments, when the policy area is characterized by greater political controversy, and when the policy area is more people-oriented.

Lowery, Konda, and Garand

David Lowery, Thomas Konda, and James Garand examine the relative ability of six models derived from the literature to account for state spending in four policy areas between 1945 and 1978.[34] The policy areas are highways, welfare, education, and health and hospitals. The six models are the autoregressive model (Davis, Dempster, and Wildavsky's incremental model), the share-of-the-pie model (Wildavsky's notion of "fair share"), the action-reaction model (budget decision makers react to the appropriations success of competitors), the resource model (spending is determined by available revenue), the constituency model (spending is a response to programmatic needs), and the leader state model (Walker's model of policy innovation).

The strongest model in all four policy areas is the autoregressive model. However, the ability of the autoregressive model to account for expenditures varies considerably across the four policy areas. Likewise, the results for the other models vary for the different policy areas. While the data support the notion that the state spending process is basically incremental, the explanatory ability of the variables does vary across policy areas.

The writers associated with this approach have provided several insights that have transformed the way the policymaking process is conceptualized. One important contribution is the emphasis on the multidimensional nature of policy. It now seems that policy outputs cannot adequately be defined in terms of a single dimension. While strong support exists for two important policy dimensions being something like Welfare-Education and Highways–Natural Resources, apparently others exist as well. How many dimensions are identified seems to be limited in large part by the number of policies included in the analysis—including both expenditure and nonexpenditure policies.

The finding that the appropriate policy model depends on the policy being examined is also important. The state policymaking process apparently cannot be portrayed by any particular model. A model that accurately describes the formulation of a specific policy will not necessarily accurately describe the shaping of other policies. The relative importance of politics and the environment will vary with the policy, or policy dimension, under consideration.

Finally, Hopkins and Weber have shown that certain policy dimensions are not accounted for by the political and environmental determinants typically employed. This calls into question the contentions of a number of earlier writers that state policies are largely determined by several key political and environmental characteristics. It suggests that a search is needed to uncover new measures that can better account for the interstate variation across these dimensions.

THE CASE FOR A CONTINGENCY APPROACH: EXPENDITURE VERSUS NONEXPENDITURE POLICIES

As was discussed in Chapter One, criticism has been directed at the conceptualization of policy outputs in expenditure terms. One of the weaknesses of such a formulation is that it works in favor of finding that environmental conditions, especially wealth, will be more important in the determination of policies than political system characteristics will be. Presumably, gross levels of expenditures will be higher in states that have more resources to channel into state activities. Seemingly, political characteristics will be more important in determining how funds are spent, and how they are distributed, than in determining the total number of dollars expended. But is there any evidence that such is the case; any evidence that the determinants of expenditure and nonexpenditure policy outputs are different?

Such evidence does indeed exist. In this section, we will look at several studies that have examined redistributive and innovative policies. But first we will examine a study that specifically compares the ability of political-structural variables to predict expenditure and nonexpenditure policy outputs, and a second study that is one of the initial attempts to define policy in nonexpenditure terms.

LeMay

Michael LeMay employs both a nonexpenditure and an expenditure output to measure state policy toward urban areas.[35] His objective is to determine whether the relative explanatory power of political-structural variables is affected by using the two types of output measures. His nonexpenditure output is an index of activity directed toward urban areas. The index is derived from responses by state officials to a questionnaire on legislative activity in fifteen areas of interest to urban areas. The expenditure output measure is the per capita expenditure for intergovernmental aid in 1966. These output measures are tested against fourteen indicators of socioeconomic and political-structural concepts.

The simple correlations between the dependent variable and the political-structural variables are all higher for the nonexpenditure output measure than for the expenditure output measure. Moreover, none of the socioeconomic measures was significantly correlated with the expenditure measure, while the nonexpenditure measure was significantly correlated with all of them. The multivariate analysis reveals a more complex relationship among the categories of variables.

LeMay includes one political system concept—party competition—and one structural concept—Grumm's legislative professionalism index—and his nonexpenditure output measure. The political and structural variables are correlated with the output measure while three of the socioeconomic concepts are held constant. When controls are employed, two of the relationships remain significant at the .05 level while the other four fall below that level, although in a couple of cases not that far below. Industrialization emerges as the strongest variable. But the relationships between party competition and professionalism and the dependent variable remain significant when income is controlled for. Moreover, these same relationships fall only slightly below significant levels when controls are employed for urbanization. While industrialization is the strongest variable, LeMay contends that the results also indicate that the political-structural variables are important determinants of nonexpenditure policies.

> The multivariate analysis confirmed that the political-structural explanatory concepts are closely related to the socioeconomic ones. But the results presented here do suggest the need to modify the "new orthodoxy" that Jacob and Vines described. While the results of the multi-

variate analysis parallel Dye's findings concerning industrialization, they modify past findings insofar as the political-structural explanatory concepts maintain significant levels of correlation with the nonexpenditure measure of output even after income is partialled out. In addition, the correlation between Grumm's Index of Professionalism and the nonexpenditure measure of output when urbanization is held constant is also high enough to indicate that a modification of the new orthodoxy may be in order.[36]

While some caveats are in order, this study suggests that the association between the political system and policy outputs can be enhanced by developing more nonexpenditure output measures. The relationships among the environment, the political system, and policy outputs seem to be conditioned by whether the dependent variable is defined in monetary or nonmonetary terms.

McCrone and Cnudde

The effort of Donald McCrone and Charles Cnudde is one of the earliest attempts to construct a nonexpenditure measure of policy.[37] An antidiscrimination scale is constructed on the basis of state legislation in the areas of public accommodations, employment, education, and housing. One environmental variable, percentage black, and one political system variable, party competition, are employed in three alternative models in an attempt to determine the interplay of environmental and political system characteristics in influencing this particular category of policy. Party competition emerges as a direct determinant of antidiscrimination legislation. The developmental sequence runs from percentage black through party competition to antidiscrimination legislation. A smaller percentage of blacks results in more party competition, which leads to the adoption of more antidiscrimination legislation. Here is an early, and generally overlooked, piece of research hinting that politics might be of greater consequence than the environment for certain types of nonexpenditure politics.

Fry and Winters

Probably no single piece of research has had greater impact on the resurrection of political variables than the work of Brian Fry and

Richard Winters.[38] Their findings provided a source of comfort for political scientists who were convinced that politics mattered in the determination of policies. Fry and Winters contend that previous research had been biased against political variables because it had examined a measure of public policy in which the influence of the political system is likely to be negligible, "that is, levels of public revenues and expenditures."[39]

To overcome this problem, they devise for their dependent variable an index that measured the redistribution of resources within the states. The index measures the ratio of expenditure benefits to tax burdens for the three lowest income classes in each state. They hypothesize that political system variables will be more important than socioeconomic variables in explaining redistributive policy. The rationale for their hypothesis harkens back to some of the more traditional writings on the determinants of public policies.

> [T]he political analyst may have to look beyond levels of taxes and expenditures to find politics having an independent or dominant influence on policy outcomes in the states. . . . As Key originally hypothesized, a fruitful area of search for such influence may be the redistributive policies of state governments.[40]

While only a few of the associations between the political and socioeconomic variables and the redistributive index are even of moderate strength, collectively the impact of the political variables is greater than that of the socioeconomic variables. The political variables account for 46 percent of the variation among the states while the socioeconomic variables account for 27 percent of the variation. While the weak associations reported mitigate against making a strong case for the influence of political characteristics in the determination of policy, the results mark a departure from most previous research. Here is at least a suggestion that politics does matter, at least in the case of redistributive policies.

While the work of Fry and Winters was welcome news to many, it was not without its critics. One of the first criticisms was offered by John L. Sullivan.[41] In effect, he accuses Fry and Winters of stacking the deck in favor of the political variables. Sullivan points out that Fry and Winters employed twelve political variables but only six socioeconomic variables. Even though they selected the five best predictors under each category, Sullivan states that this still involved comparing the best five of twelve variables with the best five of six variables. Sullivan purports to overcome this methodological short-coming by adding six socioeconomic variables to the analysis. Employing all twenty-four variables, he reverses the findings of Fry and Winters. When he selects the best five variables of each set and finally the best three variables, the results are still inconsistent with the findings of Fry and Winters. In each case, the magnitude of the relationships changes, but not the basic relationship.

In response to perceived methodological weaknesses in the formulation of Fry and Winters' index, Bernard Booms and James Halldorson reformulated the index.[42] They then examined the relationships between their revised index and the same independent variables employed in the original study. While the differences between their results and those of Fry and Winters probably are not as great as they would suggest, differences nonetheless exist (see Table 5.8). The figures in parentheses are the comparable results from Fry and Winters' study. The magnitude of virtually every relationship was increased. Also, the relationship between interparty competition and redistribution was reversed—increased party competition is now associated with greater redistribution. However, while the point is virtually ignored in their discussion, Booms and Halldorson substantiate Fry and Winters' principal finding—political variables are more important than socioeconomic variables.

Hanson

In an examination of state policies under the Aid to Families with Dependent Children Program, Russell Hanson contends that expenditure measures reveal little of the redistributive nature of policies.[43] Such measures do not reveal the policy discretion available to policymakers in determining the amount or types of assistance and the eligibility requirements for such programs. Such decisions determine how redistributive state welfare policies will be.

> This discretion is possible because a given amount of effort or expenditure may be used to purchase quite different types of welfare policy, defined in terms of their eligibility and benefit provisions. Policies with strict eligibility conditions and generous benefits may cost about the same as policies with loose eligibility requirements and meager benefits.

TABLE 5.8. Relations between Independent Variables and Booms and Halldorson's Reformulated Redistribution Index

	Hypothesized Relation	Zero-Order	Partial	Regression Coefficient	Beta Coefficient
I. Variables					
Socioeconomic variables					
Ability to pay					
Median income	+	.65 (.18)	.42 (-.27)	13.33[a]	1.11
Industrialization	+	.43 (.29)	.06 (-.02)	7.66	.05
Urbanization	+	.67 (.34)	.30 (.15)	26.21[b]	.33
Education	+	.39 (-.01)	.45 (17)	510.33[a]	.48
Need (demand)					
Gini index	+	-.43 (.00)	-.18 (.22)	-82.68	-.21
% under $3,000	+	-.56 (-.14)	.60 (-.07)	243.58[a]	2.07
Political variables					
Mass political behavior					
Political partic.	+	.34 (.14)	.40 (.37)	25.79[a]	.41
Democratic vote	+	-.30 (-.06)	.06 (.11)	5.10	.06
Interparty comp.	+	.24 (-.21)	.14 (-.14)	18.92	.08
Leg. inducements	+	.37 (.03)	-.10 (.07)	-38.95	-.07
Government insts.					
Apportionment	–	.07 (.04)	-.17 (.01)	-4.65	-.09
Leg. party cohesion	+	.50 (.24)	.20 (-.05)	1240.88	.11
Governor power	+	.52 (.26)	-.10 (.12)	-259.89	-.07
Governor tenure	+	.47 (.17)	.36 (.12)	2343.20[a]	.24
Elite Behavior					
I.G. strength	–	-.23 (-.04)	-.24 (-.17)	-2408.95	-.19
Civ. ser. coverage	+	.44 (.33)	.20 (.34)	5.46	.14
Leg. professionalism	+	.56 (.51)	.20 (.28)	2.34	.20
Innovative index	+	.70 (.46)	.41 (.07)	60.96	.44
Constant				-182305.72	

II. Multiple coefficients of determination

	R^2
All variables	.64 (.55)
Socioeconomic variables	.56 (.17)
Political variables	.72 (.38)

III. Multiple-partial coefficients of determination[c]

Political variables controlled for socioeconomic variables	.64 (.46)
Socioeconomic variables controlled for political variables	.42 (.27)

Note: Numbers in parentheses are from Fry and Winters, "The Politics of Redistribution," p. 520.

[a]Indicates significant at 5% level for a two-tailed t test. Two-tailed tests were used in order to test both the sign and the magnitude of the coefficients.

[b]Indicates significant at 10% level for a two-tailed t test.

[c]For a discussion of this statistic see Humber M. Blalock, *Social Statistics* (New York: McGraw-Hill, 1960), pp. 350-51.

Source: Bernard H. Booms and James R. Halldorson, "The Politics of Redistribution: A Reformulation," *American Political Science Review* 67 (September 1973: 930).

Similarly, the same type of welfare policy (again measured by its contents) may require substantially greater outlays in one state than it does in another because of differences in population, need, etc. Therefore the content of welfare policies, and hence their redistributive impact, cannot be accurately inferred from the cost of those policies.[44]

Hanson contends that a more realistic way of examining policies is to focus on their components; in this case, caseloads and payments. Caseloads and payments, in turn, are influenced by decisions about eligibility requirements and the size of payments. According to Hanson, state policymakers have more discretion in determining the size of payments than in determining eligibility. Policymakers can affect the size of payments in two ways. First, they can adjust the estimate of need for families standard upon which the payment is based. This is apparently done frequently. Second, they can adjust the proportion of this standard that AFDC payments will constitute. This is done less frequently, mostly because policymakers are reluctant to reduce the percentage.

Political variables are important in accounting for the variation in discretion among the states. One of those variables, as suggested by Key, is the degree of interparty competition. Also important is the bias associated with competition—the extent to which competition favors either the Democratic or Republican party. The level of federal reimbursement to the states affects both eligibility and payments, with the greater influence on payments. Interestingly, in some states, as the federal share increases state effort decreases. These states are substituting federal money for their own.

Walker

Jack Walker is concerned with explaining why some states adopt innovative policies more rapidly than others.[45] He develops an innovation score based upon the speed of adoption of eighty-eight programs in a variety of policy areas. He relates several socioeconomic and political variables to the innovation score to try to account for the interstate variation. These relationships are examined in three time periods: 1870–1929, 1900–29, 1930–66.

The more innovative states are more industrialized, more urbanized, and more populated. Also, the per capita income is higher and the value of farm land is greater. One political variable, party competition, is not consistently related to innovation. A second political variable, a measure of urban representation in the state legislature, is not related to the innovation score in the 1900–29 time period, but is related in the 1930–66 time period. Table 5.9 details the relationships between innovation and some of the political system measures, controlled for some of the socioeconomic variables. Generally, the relationships support the contention that environmental forces are more important in shaping policy outputs than are political system factors. However, the strongest partial correlation is between the David-Eisenberg index of urban representation and the composite index score. This suggests that states in which urban areas are better represented tend to be more innovative. This finding is in contrast to

TABLE 5.9. Relationships between the Composite Innovation Score and Measures of Legislative Apportionment and Party Competition

	Zero-Order	Value Added Manufac-turing	Per-cent Urban	Total Popu-lation	Per Capita Income	Four Factors Combined
Apportionment						
David-Eisenberg index	.65	.47	.64	.67	.60	.58
Schubert-Press index	.26	.12	.34	.31	.26	.21
Party competition						
Hofferbert index	.54	.35	.34	.50	.26	.12
Riley-Walker index—gov.	.40	.33	.22	.47	.09	.17
Riley-Walker index—legis.	.31	.24	.17	.34	.04	.07
Turnover in office						
Schlesinger index of opportunity	.53	.40	.39	.32	.34	.24
Legislative services						
Grumm's index of legislative professionalism	.63	.38	.33	.41	.51	.11

Source: Jack L. Walker, "The Diffusion of Innovations among the American States," *American Political Science Review* 63 (September 1969): 886.

previous studies employing an expenditure output, which generally concluded that apportionment was not an important variable in explaining policy outputs.

Walker attempts to go beyond the statistical relationships uncovered to explain how the decisions to adopt innovative policies are made. He contends that innovations diffuse among the states by a process of competition and emulation. When states are considering action in a given field, they look around to see what other states are doing in that regard. In particular, they look to states with similar characteristics. Often, this means states in the same region. They will then take cues from those states. As Walker says,

> the likelihood of a state adopting a new program is higher if other states have already adopted the idea. The likelihood becomes higher still if the innovation has been adopted by a state viewed by key decision makers as a point of legitimate comparison. Decision makers are likely to adopt new programs, therefore, when they become convinced that their state is relatively deprived, or that some need exists to which other states in their "league" have already responded.[46]

Decision makers apparently decide what league they want to play in and then compare their efforts with those of other states in that league. What other states a state decides to compare itself with can determine whether a state provides services commensurate with its resources or at a level above or below those resources. Walker produces evidence for the existence of regional groupings of states. There is a tendency for certain states to be regional pace-setters, with other states following their lead. Thus, some states take their cues from the more farsighted trend-setters and continually adopt policies later than the vanguard states. The regional groupings are not geographically perfect, suggesting that certain states, for example, New York, act as models for states in more than one region.

Professional associations of governmental officials provide the channels of communication for the exchange of information about programs among the states. Professional associations also facilitate the movement of their members to jobs in other states, which also disseminates information about programs. Increasingly, these communication channels have become more nationalized. The result is more national standards of performance, which has resulted in a weakening of the regional clusters observed in earlier eras. The overall adoption time for innovations has also been reduced. This is due mostly to quicker adoption by states that have traditionally lagged behind.

Here is some additional support for the contention that political system factors will be of importance when nonexpenditure outputs are examined. Walker is concerned not with the magnitude of spending but rather with the decision to adopt policies earlier than other states. Relationships were established between environmental characteristics and innovativeness. But a strong association existed between one measure of apportionment and innovation that persisted even when socioeconomic measures were controlled for. And this relationship strengthened over time. The emulation process described by Walker, grounded in regionalism, is similar to the regionalism political routine outlined by Sharkansky. Both stress the importance of regional consultation among officials for the policymaking process. An understanding of the process of emulation is essential if one is to grasp how the diffusion of innovative policy takes place. This technique, used by policymakers, helps to convert demands for change into new policies.

Gray

Virginia Gray examines the diffusion of innovative policies in the areas of education, welfare, and civil rights.[47] She develops and tests an interaction diffusion model. She finds that in half of the cases examined, innovations do seem to diffuse through interaction. Unlike Walker, Gray calculates innovation scores separately for each policy area. The results produced modify some of Walker's findings. States can fluctuate widely on the measure of innovation. Some of the most innovative states have not adopted some innovations and some of the least innovative states are early adopters of certain innovations. Further, innovation appears to be time-specific: states that are innovators in one time period are not necessarily innovators in another time period. Finally, with the exception of civil rights policies, states that are early adopters in a given area are not necessarily among the leaders in adopting other policies in that area.

Innovative states tend to be wealthier and to have stronger party competition. However, Gray's data do not allow for a determination of the relative influence of the two factors. Walker also found that innovative states were wealthier, but he was not able to establish a consistent relationship between party competition and innovation. Like Walker's study, Gray's research hints that political variables might be more influential in the determination of nonexpenditure policies than in the determination of expenditure policies.

Donald C. Menzel and Irwin Feller reinforce Gray's position.[48] They study technological innovation in ten state highway and air pollution agencies. They report that the early adoption of an innovation in one area is not necessarily associated with the early adoption of other innovations in that area. There is a tendency for a state to be a fast or slow adopter in one area but not both. The authors conclude that "'innovativeness' is not a general characteristic of state governments as such, but rather tends to be specific to either given technologies or given agencies."[49]

Robert Savage takes Gray to task for a methodological weakness and offers results that challenge hers.[50] Savage contends that by employing only twelve policy measures—three each in the areas of education, social welfare, and civil rights—Gray did not adequately sample potential policy areas. He attempts to correct this suggested weakness by employing 181 policy measures during three time periods: the nineteenth century, 1900–29, and 1930–70. He reports that less variation exists today among the states in rates of innovation. Some of the previously innovative states have become less so while some of the previously less innovative states have stepped up their rates of adoption.

Within this pattern of increasing similarity over time, however, some states stand out. California, Minnesota, and Ohio rank in the top quartile for all three time periods while another nine states consistently rank in the top half. At the other extreme, four states—Delaware, Georgia, Mississippi, and South Carolina—have consistently scored in the lowest quartile across the three time periods. Another seven states have consistently scored in the lower half in every period. Moreover, the most innovative states have continued to become relatively more innovative while the least innovative states have tended to become relatively less innovative.

These findings move Savage to suggest that "Gray may have been too hasty in discounting a general innovativeness trait as a variable characteristic of the American states."[51] He does hedge a bit, however, when he allows that "to argue that innovativeness is a pervasive factor in the policy actions of states does not warrant disregarding her assertion that innovativeness is, at least partially, issue- and time-specific."[52]

Gray has also concerned herself with determining the correlates of "progressivism" or "liberalism" in policy.[53] Progressivism is defined as higher levels of expenditures and greater innovation. Previous research has linked both wealth and party competition to higher spending and earlier adoption of innovations. But economic development has always been considered the key variable: wealthier states always spend at higher levels and are more innovative. Gray finds that this is not an inviolate relationship: progressivism is not a uni-dimensional factor underlying all policy. An examination of state spending in the areas of education and welfare finds that correlations among policies in the two areas are near zero or negative.

Innovation in the areas of welfare, education, and civil rights is looked at. In the area of civil rights policies, there is a tendency toward consistency in innovation. In the other two areas, innovation appears to be time-specific. Also, early innovation in an area is not associated with later higher spending in that area. When the welfare and educational policy areas are examined separately, only a moderate link exists between progressivism in expenditures and in innovation. Gray contends that these results argue for differentiating according to issue area and policy dimension—innovation versus expenditures.

Dye

A number of factors are found to be related to innovation (see Table 5.10).[54] The strongest relationships are with legislative profes-

TABLE 5.10. Correlates of Policy Innovation in the American States

Income	.56	Party Competition	.34
Urbanization	.54	Voter Participation	.28
Education	.32	Civil Service Coverage	.53
Tax Revenue	.28	Legislative Professionalism	.62

Note: Figures are simple correlation coefficients for relationships with the innovation index.

Source: Thomas R. Dye, *Understanding Public Policy*, 4th ed. (Englewood Cliffs, N.J.: Prentice-Hall, 1981), p. 361.

sionalism, civil service coverage, income, and urbanization. Further analysis of the data leads Dye to conclude that greater professionalism in the legislature and the bureaucracy is the most important direct cause of innovation. More professional legislators and bureaucrats adopt more national standards and want the most recent and best programs for their states. Also important is an educated and active citizenry. There appears to be a causal link among education, participation, and innovation. These findings give "some limited support to the pluralist contention that an educated and active political constituency can have an impact on public policy—at least to the extent that such a constituency seems to promote novelty and experimentation in programs and policies."[55]

THE CASE FOR A CONTINGENCY APPROACH: A DEVELOPMENTAL RELATIONSHIP

It was noted in Chapter Three that the association between wealth and spending has declined during the decades of this century. The impact of a particular factor, industrialization, was also shown to vary in its impact on policy outputs. This raises the possibility that the influence of socioeconomic and political system variables might not be consistent over time. The relative influence of the two categories of variables might be conditioned by when the research is conducted. Since virtually all of the comparative state policy research is cross-sectional, perhaps the results of that research are timebound.[56] Insights uncovered about the roles of the environment and the political system during the 1960s and 1970s might hold for that era but not for previous or subsequent times. For example, contemporary research minimizes the significance of political system characteristics. Perhaps that is true now but was not always so, or perhaps will not always be so.

B. Guy Peters offers preliminary evidence that such might be the case.[57] He indicates that the relationship among socioeconomic variables, political system variables, and public expenditures is curvilinear over time (see Figure 5.1).

Public policy formation consists of three developmental stages. The importance of socioeconomic and political system variables fluctuates from stage to stage. The first stage is the Traditional Stage. In this stage, the level of expenditures is influenced primarily by the

FIGURE 5.1. Hypothesized Relationships of Independent Variables to Public Policy

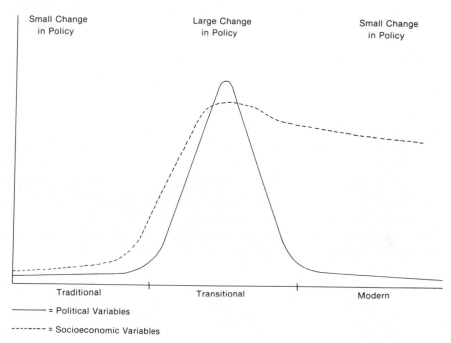

Source: B. Guy Peters, "Public Policy, Socioeconomic Conditions, and the Political System: A Note on their Developmental Relationship," *Polity* 5 (Winter 1972). 279.

attitudes of the decision makers and very little by socioeconomic conditions. The public has yet to become mobilized in any policy areas, so the desires of the policymakers will be paramount.

The second stage is the Transitional Stage, or take-off stage, during which the policy area enters a period of sustained growth. Political system variables have their greatest importance during this stage. The public becomes mobilized during this stage and begins to make demands of the decision makers. The most important variables will be those of an organizational nature, but mass participation variables will also be important in certain policy areas.

The final stage is the Modern Stage, which is basically one of reaction to environmental conditions. The major decisions on policy were made during the Transitional Stage. During the last stage, policymaking largely consists of incremental changes in existing policy. These changes are influenced by either a need for greater spending in certain areas or the availability of increased resources. The political system will have become a bureaucracy concerned principally with implementing policies.[58]

The impact of both the socioeconomic and political variables is comparatively small in the Traditional Stage. The influence of both escalates dramatically during the Transitional Stage, and then they part ways during the Modern Stage. The contribution of the socioeconomic variables stays comparably high during this last stage, while the path of the political variables drops precipitously. While political variables play their greatest role during the second stage, the socioeconomic variables are also crucial. Peters states that this is due to the necessity of adequate resources to support the policies favored by the decision makers. This second stage is also characterized by large changes in policy. These changes are responses to new demands. After this stage, changes tend to be of an incremental nature. During the Modern Stage,

> changes in expenditures will be a function of changes in the availability of resources. The political system could be said to have decided what percentage of changes in the resource base it will take for its purposes during the take-off period. After that point, the changes in expenditures should be functions simply of the changes in resources.[59]

Peters tests his conceptualization of the policy process using data from the United Kingdom from 1850 to 1965, and from Sweden from 1865 to 1965. He finds some support for his argument, particularly in the United Kingdom. If the same forces were at work in the American States, this might account for the way that the determinants of public policies are perceived.

> The results provide one interpretation of the consistent finding of the lack of relationship between political conditions and public policy outcomes. Especially in the context of the American states, it can be said that many of the significant decisions regarding policy outputs were made prior to the times at which the cross-sectional analyses were done. In those policy areas, the states had already passed into the "modern" period during which policy decisions are primarily incremental and based on the availability of resources. Examination of the same policy areas in different time periods might produce quite different results, such as the ones presented here.[60]

THE CASE FOR A CONTINGENCY APPROACH: CROSS-SECTIONAL ANALYSIS VERSUS TIME-SERIES ANALYSIS

While not specifically weighing the relative influence of environmental and political system variables, Virginia Gray's research nonetheless offers insights and warnings to those who do wrestle with such questions.[61] She examines several policies related to the have–have-not struggle. And, like Sharkansky, she employs only measures of state expenditures. Two models are used, one representing the environment and one the political system. The environmental model is called "economic resources" and is measured by per capita income. The political model is labeled "competitive threat" and is measured by competition and turnout. Both models are examined with cross-sectional and time-series data. The underlying assumption is that more competition or economic resources, at any time or over time, will result in a higher level of have-not policies.

The results for the competitive threat model indicate that the impact of political variables is stronger when measured over time. Also, different relationships between competition and turnout and the various policies exist between the cross-sectional and time-series data. The findings for the economic resources model are similar. Again, the correlations are of greater magnitude for the time-series rather than the cross-sectional data. But the relationships between per capita income and the policies examined are more consistent at one point in time and over time than was the case with the two variables employed to test the competitive threat model.

This research has at least two implications for the comparative study of state policymaking. First, apparently the relative impact of political variables can be increased by examining policymaking over time rather than at a particular point in time. Second, the results of cross-sectional and time-series studies can differ and inferences should be drawn from one type of study only at risk. In this study, if inferences had been drawn from the cross-sectional data, such conclusions would have been incorrect in eight of eighteen cases. Since most of the policymaking research at the state level has employed cross-sectional data, possibly much of the conventional wisdom in this area is less well-grounded than many suppose.

AN ALTERNATIVE MODEL TO POLITICS
VERSUS THE ENVIRONMENT

Jeff Stonecash charges that the entire discussion of the relative importance of socioeconomic and political variables is predicated on faulty theory. In his theoretical reformulation, he states forthrightly:

> This essay argues that the models used in most of these analyses did not test our theoretical notions of the role of politics and wealth, and so the results are largely meaningless. The issue of relative statistical importance (i.e., of independent effects of politics and wealth) involved an inappropriate theoretical question answered by misspecified empirical analyses. The problem has not been the selection of policy areas, or the types of dependent variables used, but the theory specification employed.[62]

According to Stonecash, both politics and wealth should be conceptualized as facilitative factors. Neither politics nor wealth "causes" policy outputs. Politics intervenes between demands and policies. Without the political process, there would likely not be a link between demands and policies. But politics, while a necessary condition for such a linkage, is not a sufficient condition. For example, certain demands could be ignored. Also, variations in the political process are likely to produce variations in the conversion of inputs into outputs. The role of wealth is also indirect. The ability of any political system to adopt expenditure policies depends on the resources available. Greater wealth provides greater discretion to policymakers.

Policy is not likely to exist without public demand. Once demand exists, then politics and wealth act as intervening variables between public preferences and policies. In terms of a causal sequence, demand occurs first.

> Policy making may reflect both preferences of the population (demands) and independent activity of politicians and bureaucrats (withinputs). In this case, political system characteristics (e.g., congressmen's reelection goals) would be sufficient to "cause" policy. Thus politics can act both as a necessary condition for a relationship between preferences and policy, and as a sufficient condition for policy levels. The relative significance of each of these roles must be established empirically.[63]

Figure 5.2 portrays Stonecash's conceptualization of the relationship between preference and policy expenditures as mediated by

**FIGURE 5.2. The Effects of Politics and Wealth on
Preference-Demand Relationships**

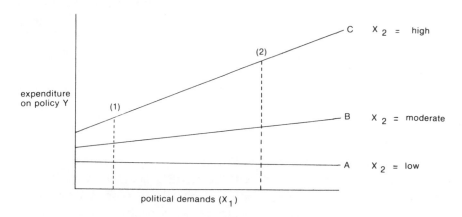

Source: Jeff Stonecash, "Assessing the Roles of Politics and Wealth for Public Policy," *Political Methodology* 6 (1979): 467.

politics and wealth. Line A represents political systems that do not convert preferences into demands. Lines B and C represent political systems that are moderately and highly responsive to preferences, respectively.

> As the graph shows, in situations where public demand is low (1), a highly facilitative political system will not produce high public policy levels. In situations where preference levels are high (2), public policy will be high only if the necessary condition of a facilitative political system exists (line C). Where these conditions do not exist (line A), demands will not produce high public policy levels. Wealth variations also produce variations in conversion patterns. If a set of political units had equivalent political system characteristics (say, Line B) and one set had higher wealth levels than the units on Line B, then the effect would be to shift line B upward, making a line that is either parallel or has a different slope. The effects of political system and wealth characteristics, then, are to produce (for equivalent demand variations) conversion patterns with different slopes and heights.[64]

Different conversion patterns are expected for differing political system characteristics and levels of wealth.

Stonecash is critical of previous studies that have grouped together a variety of political system characteristics. He contends that there are two distinct categories of political variables—those related to the response bias of the system and those related to the capability of the system to implement policies. Bias refers to the fact that existing political structures and processes advantage certain interests and disadvantage others. The result is that all demands do not have an equal chance to be heard. Implementation refers to the execution of policy once it has been enacted. The successful implementation of policy requires, among other things, competent, willing administrators, sufficient authority to carry out the policy, and adequate resources. During the implementation stage, policy can be significantly altered, or even blocked. Stonecash suggests that bias is probably of greater consequence for distributive or redistributive policies while the capability to implement is probably more important for less distributive policies.

The model was tested by analyzing two policy areas—Aid to Families with Dependent Children and Medicaid programs.[65] Demand was measured by an index of fundamentalism in religious attitudes. The inverse of this index yielded an index of liberalism in public attitudes toward policy. Median family income was the indicator of wealth, and the political system was represented by Schlesinger's index of the governor's formal powers. The policy indicators were the average monthly AFDC payment and an index indicating the number of Medicaid services provided by the state and the percentage of the state's population that was eligible to receive such services.

As postulated, stronger policy preferences were associated with higher levels of the policies. Moreover, heightened response was associated with greater wealth and stronger formal powers for the governor.

> There is not, then, some invariant relationships between culture and policy. That relationship is contingent on the resources available, and the concentration of formal authority in the political system. The significance of wealth and political conditions is that they produce these variations in conversion patterns.[66]

Reinforcement for Stonecash's theory is provided by Grumm and Dye. Grumm finds that certain structural characteristics tend to reinforce inputs from the environment.[67] The strongest relationship is between legislative professionalism and welfare liberalism. Weaker relationships were discovered between apportionment and state educational policy, and between party competition and welfare policy, under certain economic conditions.

Dye also focuses on the role of the political system. He recently urged that politics be viewed as facilitating the conversion of demands into outputs rather than as causing policy outputs.

> If we accept this view, we would not really expect variations in political systems—variations in competition, participation, partisanship, reformism, and such—to directly cause public policy. Instead, we would expect variations in political systems to affect relationships between demands and resources and public policies. For example, we would not expect highly competitive political systems to produce different policies than noncompetitive systems, but instead we might inquire whether the relationships between population characteristics and public policy are closer in competitive than in noncompetitive systems. Our focus would shift to the impact of political system variables on relationships between environmental conditions (measures of demands and resources) and public policies.[68]

SUMMARY

Several alternative ways of understanding the interrelationships among the socioeconomic environment, the political system, and policy outputs have been presented. The traditional view, characterized by the early efforts of Dawson and Robinson and Dye, held that policy was largely determined by the socioeconomic characteristics of the states. The influence of the political system was minimal. Sharkansky and Morehouse argue for the preeminence of the political system. Other work suggests that the traditional view is accurate only under certain conditions.

One of the reformulations holds that the influence of the environment might be greater for certain policies but not for others. Policies, and also the environment and the political system, apparently are multidimensional. The most appropriate model to describe the policy process might vary with the policy area under examination. In particular, nonexpenditure policies seem to be more heavily influenced by political factors. It has also been suggested that the relative influence of the environment and the political system might vary over time. Perhaps at different stages of the development of the policy process the relative impact of the two might vary. Finally, it has been argued that the most realistic way to conceptualize the environment and the political system is as facilitative factors. Policy is produced by a given level of demand being mediated by political characteristics and varying levels of wealth.

NOTES

1. Richard E. Dawson and James A. Robinson, "Inter-Party Competition, Economic Variables, and Welfare Policies in the American States," *Journal of Politics* 25 (May 1963): 265–89.

2. Richard I. Hofferbert, "The Relation between Public Policy and Some Structural and Environmental Variables in the American States," *American Political Science Review* 60 (March 1966): 73–82.

3. Ibid., p. 73.

4. Ibid., p. 82.

5. Ibid.

6. Sarah McCally Morehouse, *State Politics, Parties and Policy* (New York: Holt, Rinehart and Winston, 1981), p. 37.

7. Thomas R. Dye, *Politics, Economics, and the Public: Policy Outcomes in the American States* (Chicago: Rand McNally, 1966), p. 293.

8. Ibid., p. 296.

9. Michael Lewis-Beck, "The Relative Importance of Socioeconomic and Political Variables in Public Policy," *American Political Science Review* 71 (June 1977): 559–66.

10. Ibid., p. 566.

11. Charles Lindblom, "The Science of Muddling Through," *Public Administration Review* 19 (Spring 1959): 79–88.

12. Aaron Wildavsky, *The Politics of the Budgetary Process* (Boston: Little, Brown, 1964).

13. Ira Sharkansky, *Spending in the American States* (Chicago: Rand McNally, 1978), p. 73.

14. Ibid., pp. 151–52.

15. Ibid., p. 152.

16. Morehouse, *State Politics.*

17. Ibid., p. 365.

18. Ibid., p. 417.

19. Ibid., p. 482.

20. Charles F. Cnudde and Donald J. McCrone, "Party Competition and Welfare Policies in the American States," *American Political Science Review* 63 (September 1969): 858–66.

21. Ibid., p. 865.

22. Robert E. Crew, Jr., "Dimensions of Public Policy: A Factor Analysis of State Expenditures," *Social Science Quarterly* 50 (September 1969): 381–88.

23. The assumption underlying factor analysis is that variables that are highly interrelated have certain common traits, or factors. The principal factors extracted from the analysis are groups of variables that are highly correlated with each other, but weakly correlated, or not correlated, with other groups of variables. The correlation coefficient between a variable and the factor is called a loading. The stronger the relationship between a variable and the traits underlying the factor, the higher the loading. Variables with the highest loadings come closest to representing the underlying traits. An examination of the variables with the highest loadings on a factor enables one to determine the factor's underlying traits and thus to assign a label to that factor.

24. Crew, "Dimensions of Public Policy," p. 383.

25. Ibid., p. 385.

26. Ibid., p. 386.

27. Ibid., p. 388.

28. Ira Sharkansky and Richard I. Hofferbert, "Dimensions of State Politics, Economics, and Public Policy," *American Political Science Review* 63 (September 1969): 867–79.

29. Ibid., p. 878.

30. Anne H. Hopkins and Ronald E. Weber, "Dimensions of Public Policies in the American States," *Polity* 8 (Spring 1976): 475–89.

31. Herbert B. Asher and Donald S. Van Meter, *Determinants of Public Welfare Policies: A Causal Approach.* (Beverly Hills: Sage Professional Papers in American Politics, Vol. 1, Series No. 04–009, 1973).

32. Ibid., p. 44.

33. Yong Hyo Cho and H. George Frederickson, *Determinants of Public Policy in the American States* (Beverly Hills: Sage Professional Papers in Administrative and Policy Studies, vol. 1, series no. 03–012, 1973).

34. David Lowery, Thomas Konda, and James Garand, "Spending in the States: A Test of Six Models," *Western Political Quarterly* 37 (March 1984): 48–66.

35. Michael LeMay, "Expenditure and Nonexpenditure Measures of State Urban Policy Output: A Research Note," *American Politics Quarterly* 1 (October 1973): 511–28.

36. Ibid., p. 525.

37. Donald J. McCrone and Charles F. Cnudde, "On Measuring Public Policy," in *State Politics: Readings on Political Behavior*, ed. Robert E. Crew (Belmont, Cal.: Wadsworth, 1968), pp. 523–30.

38. Brian R. Fry and Richard F. Winters, "The Politics of Redistribution," *American Political Science Review* 64 (June 1970): 508–22.

39. Ibid., p. 508.

40. Ibid., p. 510.

41. John L. Sullivan, "A Note on Redistributive Politics," *American Political Science Review* 66 (December 1972): 1301–5.

42. Bernard H. Booms and James R. Halldorson, "The Politics of Redistribution: A Reformulation," *American Political Science Review* 67 (September 1973): 924–33.

43. Russell L. Hanson, "The 'Content' of Welfare Policy: The States and Aid to Families with Dependent Children," *Journal of Politics* 45 (August 1983): 771-85.

44. Ibid., pp. 772-73.

45. Jack L. Walker, "The Diffusion of Innovations among the American States," *American Political Science Review* 63 (September 1969): 880-99.

46. Ibid., p. 897.

47. Virginia Gray, "Innovation in the States: A Diffusion Study," *American Political Science Review* 67 (December 1973): 1174-85.

48. Donald C. Menzel and Irwin Feller, "Leadership and Interaction Patterns in the Diffusion of Innovations among the American States," *Western Political Quarterly* 30 (December 1977): 528-36.

49. Ibid., p. 536.

50. Robert L. Savage, "Policy Innovativeness as a Trait of American States," *Journal of Politics* 40 (February 1978): 212-19.

51. Ibid., p. 218.

52. Ibid.

53. Virginia Gray, "Expenditures and Innovation as Dimensions of Progressivism: A Note on the American States," *American Journal of Political Science* 18 (November 1974): 693-99.

54. Thomas R. Dye, *Understanding Public Policy*, 4th ed. (Englewood Cliffs, N.J.: Prentice-Hall, 1981), pp. 358-61.

55. Ibid., p. 361.

56. For a methodological discussion of the use of time in comparative state studies, see Harvey J. Tucker, "It's About Time: The Use of Time in Cross-sectional State Policy Research," *American Journal of Political Science* 26 (February 1982): 176-96.

57. B. Guy Peters, "Public Policy, Socioeconomic Conditions, and the Political System: A Note on Their Developmental Relationship," *Polity* 5 (Winter 1972): 277-84.

58. Ibid., p. 278.

59. Ibid., p. 280.

60. Ibid., p. 282.

61. Virginia Gray, "Models of Comparative State Politics: A Comparison of Cross-Sectional and Time Series Analysis," *American Journal of Political Science* 20 (May 1976): 235-56.

62. Jeff Stonecash, "Assessing the Roles of Politics and Wealth for Public Policy," *Political Methodology* 6 (1979): 463.

63. Ibid., p. 466.

64. Ibid., p. 467.

65. Jeff Stonecash and Susan W. Hayes, "The Sources of Public Policy: Welfare Policy in the American States," *Policy Studies Journal* 5 (Spring 1981): 681-98.

66. Ibid., p. 693.

67. John G. Grumm, "The Effects of Legislative Structure on Legislative Performance," in *State and Urban Politics: Readings in Comparative Public Policy*, ed. Richard I. Hofferbert and Ira Sharkansky (Boston: Little, Brown, 1971), pp. 298-322.

68. Dye, *Understanding Public Policy*, 4th ed., p. 333.

6

STATE PUBLIC POLICYMAKING: TWO DECADES OF ANALYSIS

To summarize twenty years of research into state public policy-making in a short book undoubtedly understates the progress that has been made in understanding how states determine policy. In two decades, political scientists and others have tested empirically many propositions initially suggested by Key, Fenton, Lockard, and others. The empirical data have confirmed some of the propositions, partially substantiated others, and rejected still others. Our understanding of state policymaking has been substantially advanced. Much remains unknown, however, about the policymaking process in the American states. Moreover, much of the empirical analysis has led to conflicting findings. We are told in one study that a given set of relationships exists; in another study, we are informed that the original suppositions are incorrect. Sorting out all of the results can be a complicated, confusing process.

One of the clearest conclusions that emerges from a bewildering array of studies is the tentative nature of most of the results. The diversity of the empirical studies argues against making assertions too strongly. Many of the generalizations derived from the literature could be better labeled "extreme generalizations." Part of the problem is that concepts are not measured consistently. It is difficult to develop a theory of public policymaking in the states when concepts are measured differently. For example, what is called party competition could be measured with different variables by different analysts. It is difficult to synthesize a number of studies purporting to deal with the same concept when that concept is operationalized in different ways. Compounding that problem is the fact that the studies are conducted in different time periods. Relationships that are true in one time period might not hold true in a different time period. Finally, the dependent variable is not consistently measured. Frequently, policy outputs are measured in expenditure terms, but at other times they are measured in nonexpenditure terms. If policy is defined in terms of expenditures it might be exclusively state spending or a combination of state and local spending. Total governmental expenditures could be examined or expenditures in particular policy areas. For all of these reasons, caution is in order when interpreting results.

With few exceptions, by selectively choosing studies one could make a case for or against particular variables. In most cases, conflicting findings have been reported. This fact again points up the danger of being incautious in forging generalizations.

By necessity, because it has been the central focus of most of the comparative state research, any summary of the state policymaking literature must return to the politics-environment controversy. A thorough reading of the previous few chapters should make one aware that there are no simple conclusions. The relationships among the environment, the political system, and policy outputs are complex. At best, relationships exist for certain areas during certain time periods. The contingency approaches discussed in Chapter Five would seem to be the most realistic view, especially the alternative model offered by Stonecash.

Environment matters, but so does politics. To talk about politics or the environment assumes that either one independently can determine policy, and that is clearly fallacious. They operate in tandem; they are inseparable. State policymakers must balance both economic and political concerns when determining policy. Policies cannot be pursued without resources, but neither do policies magically appear in the presence of resources. Policymakers must take account of resources while weighing personal desires and the demands of party, constituency, and interest groups. It is becoming increasingly clear from the empirical data that neither politics nor the environment independently determines policy. It is also increasingly apparent that neither one is necessarily always of greater relative importance.

The policymaking process is obviously not devoid of politics. Quite the contrary, it is the quintessential political process. Policy proposals are not always adopted on their merits; they are adopted because they receive more political support than competing proposals. Sometimes they are supported for reasons that are economically or even morally unsound. Nonetheless, they are adopted once they receive the requisite number of votes. Political expediency often outweighs reason and logic. So to talk about politics as being inconsequential in the policymaking process is foolish and grossly in error. In the case of the empirical lack of support for politics, inadequate measurement of political concepts is a primary culprit.

But socioeconomic factors also enter into the equation. Demands for policy arise in part because of a state's level of socioeconomic development. Groups of citizens who feel that their state is somehow deprived socially or economically will begin to press demands to remedy the situation. Policymakers must also take the level of socioeconomic development into account as they debate policy proposals. In the absence of adequate resources at the state level, or absent federal aid as compensation, states will not be able to pursue some policies.

What the exact mixture of politics and the environment will be depends on what policy area is being examined and how the environment, the political system, and policy outputs are being measured. We must be willing to accept that different policies can have different determinants. We must avoid seeking explanations that hold for all policies at all times. Rather, let us be more specific. Let us state that results apply simply to a specific policy area in a particular time period in a particular set of states. Such results would probably be less exciting, but would probably be more academically accurate and honest. Such an approach would also facilitate the development of a theory of state policymaking by clearly stipulating the conditions under which given results apply.[1]

It is not hard to understand why politics versus the environment has captured the attention of political scientists. Naturally, political scientists are concerned with assessing the role played by politics in the determination of policy, and once economics was declared to be paramount, it was inevitable that more effort would be directed toward attempting to redress the balance. Perhaps, however, too much effort has been devoted to the politics-environment issue. The result, in some cases, has been an unrealistic conceptualization of the policymaking process.

This unrealistic conceptualization is probably best manifested by the mainstream model. The model suggests the conveyor belt theory of policymaking. Elements move steadily along the conveyor belt from that part of the model labeled "environment" to that part labeled "outputs." This is not a realistic depiction of the policymaking process. A model should be an abstraction of reality, not a substitute for it. If the policymaking process is analogous to a conveyor belt, it is a belt that runs hesitatingly and is subject to frequent mechanical breakdowns. Some of the policy boxes do move smoothly from one end of the belt to the other; others are somehow lost along the route and never found; others are opened for inspection along the route and have their contents slightly altered; others are opened for inspection along the route and have their contents significantly altered; others are knocked off the belt and smashed beyond repair.

The systems model has served political scientists well for the past twenty years. Guided by this model, students of comparative state politics have gained many insights into the policymaking process. But experience with the model has enabled weaknesses to be discovered. These were documented at length in Chapter One. Research results have likewise suggested modifications. A reformulated model of the state policymaking process, based on the results of twenty years of empirical analysis, is offered in Figure 6.1. Listed under various components of the model are concepts that have been of importance in the literature.

The model adopts a longitudinal approach to policymaking. Policy outputs that emerge at a particular time represent an accretion of policy over time. Typically, policy does not spring forth totally new and without antecedents. Policy tends to develop slowly, in response to needs not satisfied by previous policy. This incremental process involves constantly modifying existing policy; generally, policymakers do not attempt at any one time to resolve a problem for all time. Even if they could agree on the nature of the problem and the best solution to that problem, they probably could not adopt and implement such a policy, owing to a lack of resources or political support. As a result, policymakers, as Sharkansky observes, tend to rely on tensions to tell them something is wrong.[2] In the absence of such tensions, policymakers tend not to act. When they do act, it is generally to make marginal adjustments to existing policy.

It is crucial that policymaking be viewed as a process that takes place over time. The policymaking process cannot be understood totally unless one is aware of this fact. Cross-sectional analysis of policymaking reveals only part of the process. The results of such

FIGURE 6.1. A Model of the State Policymaking Process

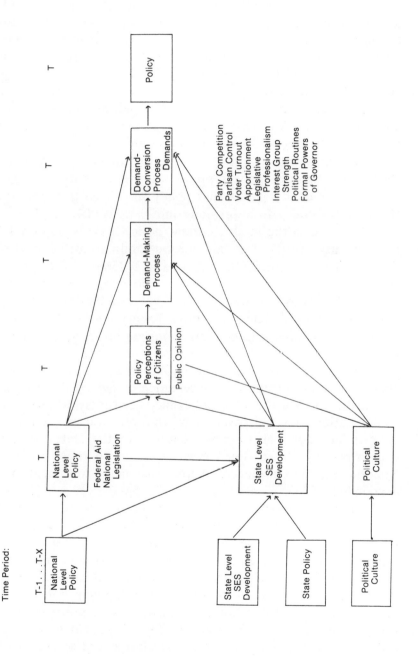

research offer insights into the determinants of policies during a given period of years. While such information is certainly useful, such an approach suffers in at least two ways. First, there is the danger of assuming that the determinants of policy uncovered in one time period are always the determinants of policy. Hofferbert's findings regarding his industrialization factor should disabuse anyone of any such notion. Cross-sectional studies merely provide a snapshot of time; to assume more is incorrect. Second, an emphasis on cross-sectional research can lead to an unrealistic conceptualization of the policymaking process. Policymaking could be viewed as discontinuous, starting de novo during each period under examination rather than as an ongoing, evolving process. The time period heading at the top of the model suggests that policy in a given time period (T) is the legacy of policy from previous time periods (T–1 . . . T–X).

According to the model, current policy is derived not only from previous state policy, but also previous and current national policy. Policies of the national government and federal aid affect state policies. As Rose has pointed out, state options can be circumscribed by national legislation. State policymakers can be forced to legislate within guidelines detailed by national lawmakers. Conditions attached to federal aid also impose limitations on state policymakers. The increasing influence of federal aid on state policymaking has been alluded to several times previously. Acceptance of federal money is almost always contingent on acceptance of federal restrictions. It is unrealistic to view the state policymaking process as not influenced by the national level of government. In a very real way, states are not independent political systems. Neither are the states severely circumscribed by the national government at all times on all issues. Nonetheless, the influence of the national government must be acknowledged.

State level socioeconomic development is also of consequence in the policymaking process. While the politics-environment debate may be misguided, and while the impact of the environment may have been overstated in some previous works, socioeconomic conditions have a vital impact on policymaking. The model demonstrates that a state's current level of socioeconomic development is determined by its previous level of development, previous state policy, and current and previous national legislation and federal aid. Citizens' policy perceptions and demands for policies are influenced by such socioeconomic factors as levels of income and industrialization. It was also documented in Chapter Two that certain political structural and process characteristics are influenced by the level of socioeconomic development. Moreover, one important element of socioeconomic development, wealth, is certainly a crucial consideration for policymakers.

The model also indicates that political culture is an important factor in the determination of policy. Political culture affects how citizens and leaders view the political system, define the proper role of government, define what options are viewed as legitimate, and define their proper role in the political system. Interstate cultural differences must be considered as a determinant of public policies.

National-level policy, state-level socioeconomic development and political culture do not directly influence policy. They are mediated by several crucial linkages. The first is the policy perceptions of citizens. Collectively, this is referred to as public opinion. The adequacy of existing policies and the most crucial problems needing attention by policymakers are not objectively obvious. These represent subjective judgments by individual citizens. All citizens in a particular state will not share common perceptions. Neither will citizens in several states confronted by apparently similar socioeconomic situations and political cultures. In both cases, perceptions will differ on the adequacy of existing policies and what are the most pressing needs. But before demands are made of policymakers, there must exist a perception on the part of a sizable portion of the citizenry that a particular problem requires the attention of policymakers. As Hopkins has described, exactly what percentage of the public must desire a particular course of action before the policy is adopted varies by time and issue.

The next step is the process of demand making. Interest groups and political parties could play an important role in this process. After the public, or more exactly, a portion of the public, perceives a policy problem as meriting the attention of policymakers, demands are made. Demand making can be conditioned by national-level policy, socioeconomic development, and political culture. The ultimate fate of such demands is uncertain. Depending on the political resources and legitimacy of the demand makers, policymakers might adopt a policy that substantially incorporates provisions sought by the demand makers, adopt but modify to some degree the demand makers' requests, or totally ignore the demand.

Next comes the demand-conversion process. As was just discussed, not all demands are converted into policies. Those demands that receive the most political support, for whatever reasons, will be enacted into policy. The conversion process can be influenced by partisan considerations, the level of voter turnout, how well-apportioned and professional the legislature is, interest group strength, the formal powers of the governor, and a variety of political routines. The model also notes that demands can originate with the policymakers—what Easton refers to as "withinputs." All policy demands do not have to originate with the public.

When converting demands into policy, policymakers can be influenced by national policy, socioeconomic development, and political culture. Previous and present national policies can set limits within which policymakers must operate. The political routine of incrementalism guarantees that previous state policy will also be a consideration. Resources must also be taken into account—some policies cannot be pursued because the resources required for their execution are not present. Money is an obvious resource, but not the only one. Adequate personnel, knowledge, and physical resources are others.

This reformulated model is more complex than the mainstream model and would be more difficult to test. But it is probably more realistic. The mainstream model suggests a process by which environmental characteristics are somehow transformed into policy outputs. The actual policymaking process is much more complex, subject to many more forces. The present model incorporates some of the factors that empirical research has found to be important.

Much has been learned about how policy is made in the American states, but much still remains to be learned. As greater responsibilities are being heaped upon the states, it is more important than ever before to understand the factors that help to shape state policies. The comparative approach to the study of state policymaking still has great utility. As more and more Americans move from the North and Northeast to the South and Southwest, and as the sunbelt states continue to become more urban and more industrial, the American states will have even more characteristics in common. Why these increasingly similar states continue to adopt policies that vary should continue to hold the interest of political scientists.

Emphasis should be placed on determining how environmental and political factors jointly shape policy rather than on the two categories of variables as competitors. One old challenge will continue to be timely—to better measure the concepts employed, including policy. If the interest generated during the past twenty years is sustained, the next twenty years should add significantly to our knowledge about the determinants of public policy in the American states.

NOTES

1. For a discussion of this and other methodological problems, see George D. Greenberg, Jeffrey A. Miller, Lawrence B. Mohr, and Bruce C. Vladeck, "Developing Public Policy Theory: Perspectives from Empirical Research," *American Political Science Review* 71 (December 1977): 1532–43.

2. Ira Sharkansky, *Public Administration: Agencies, Policies, and Politics* (New York: Freeman, 1982), pp. 229–34.

INDEX

NAME INDEX

SUBJECT INDEX

Air pollution policy, 4
American National Election Study, 63
Anglo-Saxon common law, 8
Antidiscrimination policy. *See* Civil
 rights policy
Apportionment. *See* Legislative appor-
 tionment

Budgetary process, 111–119

Capital punishment, 48, 49
Causation, 19–20
Citizens' perceptions of environmental
 conditions, 15–16, 182
Civil rights policy, 48, 72, 82, 91, 96,
 109, 148, 156, 163, 165
Comparative approach to state policymaking, 8–11
Contingency approaches: a developmental relationship, 166–168; an
 alternative model to politics versus the environment, 170–173;
 competing models and multidi-
 mensionality, 142–154; cross-
 sectional analysis versus time-
 series analysis, 169; expenditure
 versus nonexpenditure policies,
 154–166
Conveyor belt theory of policy making,
 180
Corporate income tax, 68
Criticism of the mainstream model.
 See Systems model
Cross-sectional studies, 20
Cultural lag. *See* Political culture

Demands. *See* Systems model
Democratic theory, 47

Developmental model, 143
Divided government and policymaking, 89–90

Earmarked funds, 18
Ecological variables, definition of, 7–8
Education policy, 1, 4, 54, 59, 60, 70,
 71, 81, 82, 91, 97, 100, 109, 121,
 135, 136, 141, 146, 148, 163,
 165
Environment: case for the preeminence
 of the socioeconomic environment, 132–136; definition of, 7;
 direct influence on policy, 10, 11,
 19–20, 21–22, 45–77; influence
 on policy over time, 67–71; link
 established between environment
 and policy, 45–46; relative influence on policy, 131–176. *See also*
 Systems model
Environmental variables, definition of,
 7

FAIIR criteria, 36–38. *See also* Legislative professionalism
Federal aid: dollar amounts, 1, 53;
 influence on policy, 53–58, 68,
 70–73, 112–113, 182
Feedback. *See* Systems model
Formal powers of the governor: determinants of, 34–35; influence
 on policy, 120, 122

General sales tax, 68
Gini coefficient, 31, 35
Governmental expenditures: domestic,
 by level of government, 2–3;
 policy area, by level of govern-

ABOUT THE AUTHOR

JACK M. TREADWAY received his B.S. degree from Wisconsin State University-Whitewater, his M.A. from Arizona State University, and his Ph.D. from the University of Kansas (1977). He is presently Professor of Political Science at Kutztown University where he teaches courses in Public Policy Analysis, State and Local Government, Political Parties, and Public Administration. His current research interests are the changing role of state governments and the factors influencing change in form of urban government.